W9-AVM-831

fine Gardening

EASY-TO-GROW VEGETABLES

EASY-TO-GROW VEGETABLES

GREENS, TOMATOES, PEPPERS & MORE

FROM THE EDITORS & CONTRIBUTORS
OF *FINE GARDENING*

The Taunton Press

The Taunton Press, Inc.
63 South Main Street, PO Box 5506
Newtown, CT 06470-5506
e-mail: tp@taunton.com

Editors: Jennifer Renjilian Morris, Tim Stobierski
Copy Editor: Valerie Cimino
Indexer: Cathy Goddard
Cover design: Kim Adis
Interior design: Kim Adis
Layout: Alison Wilkes

The following names/manufacturers appearing in *Fine Gardening Easy-to-Grow Vegetables* are trademarks: EarthWay®, Mirai®, Tabasco®

Library of Congress Cataloging-in-Publication Data

Fine gardening easy-to-grow vegetables : greens, tomatoes, peppers & more / editors & contributors of Fine gardening.
    pages cm
Includes index.
ISBN 978-1-63186-262-5
1. Vegetable gardening. I. Fine gardening. II. Title: Easy to grow vegetables.
SB321.F56 2016
635--dc23
                        2015034206

Printed in the United States of America
10 9 8 7 6 5 4 3 2 1

ACKNOWLEDGMENTS

Thanks to the many contributors—authors, photographers, illustrators, and editors—to Fine Gardening *magazine. Thanks to the book's editors: Jennifer Renjilian Morris, for all of her hard work putting this book together, and Timothy Stobierski, for overseeing the project.*

CONTENTS

INTRODUCTION

I CONSIDER MYSELF ONE OF THE LUCKY ONES BECAUSE MY FAMILY actually had a vegetable garden while I was growing up. And, although I hated to be assigned the chore of weeding it, I quickly learned to appreciate the fact that fresh, homegrown food tasted better than anything you could buy at the grocery store.

We had a vegetable garden for several reasons: to save money, to know exactly where our food came from and how it was raised, and to become a little more self-sufficient. It wasn't until I was an adult, however, that I would truly understand all the hard work that went into taking a small seedling and nurturing it into a plant filled with ripe tomatoes. In my own garden, I've discovered that vegetable gardening isn't easy. Luckily (for me and you), this book is filled with sage advice that will help you get the harvest of your dreams—all without breaking the bank or your back. The farmers, gardeners, and plant experts in this book will help you select the right varieties for your region, amend your soil properly, battle pests and diseases organically, and ultimately teach you when your bounty is ready to be picked.

Whether you're looking to build a small raised bed in the driveway or cultivate an acre in the backyard, the pages that follow will guide you every step of the way. And, hopefully, someday your kids will be like me—happy that their parents took the time and effort to tend a vegetable garden.

—Danielle Sherry is senior editor of Fine Gardening

BASICS

FINDING SPACE
FOR VEGGIES

All you need to grow your favorite edibles is a sunny place. The best part? The spot can be as small as the corner of a balcony or as big as your backyard. Just follow kitchen-garden designer Sarah Bush's techniques to fit your veggies in anywhere.

LATELY, THERE SEEMS TO BE A LOT OF FARMER ENVY IN THE gardening world. The recent locavore (eating locally grown food) trend, food-contamination scares, and the high price of produce have many grasping the shovel and looking at their lawns with a hungry gleam in their eye. Self-sufficiency and the desire to grow our own food for pleasure and health is appealing, but not all of us have a lawn that we can convert into a big vegetable garden. If you work creatively within your means, however, you might find that the joys of a small-space veggie garden far outweigh the expense and hard work of a larger garden. Whether your limited resources include a tiny patch of earth, a sunny driveway or balcony, or the existing landscape around your home, you can use the following techniques to get up close and personal with your food supply. As a bonus, you'll find that it's much easier to stay on top of weeding, watering, and pest management if your crops are a reasonable size.

Get creative to overcome your lack of land. Bright red oil-drum containers can find the perfect home on a balcony or in a back alley while providing crispy lettuce and delicious eggplants for the dinner table.

THE SALAD-BAR GARDEN

A small bed, like this 6-foot-long and 4-foot-wide garden, can produce enough fresh produce for a daily salad. Harvesting starts in early spring and continues through fall.

THE PLANTS

1 CURLY PARSLEY • 2 plants

Curly parsley forms small mounded tufts, which are the perfect shape to round out the sharp edges of the bed. This herb is an excellent green to add to a salad.

2 STRAWBERRIES • 4 plants

A few strawberry plants go a long way after producing runners, which cascade over the edges of the bed. By the second year, these few plants will produce several pints of berries.

3 THYME • 4 plants

Because it is a drought-tolerant plant, thyme does well as a filler between the aggressive, thirsty strawberry plants. Use it fresh in salads for a pungent snap, or cooked with fish or poultry.

4 MARIGOLDS • 4 plants

Marigold flowers taste like lemon and tolerate hot conditions and low amounts of water—perfect for a sidewalk raised bed.

5 SWISS CHARD • 9 plants

Swiss chard is a good source of summer greens. It lasts longer than lettuce and keeps producing well into fall. The bright stems hold their color when cooked.

6 SUNFLOWERS • 6 plants

Tall sunflowers, with their edible seeds and petals, provide needed shade to the salad greens below. Trellised indeterminate tomatoes could also be used.

RAISED BEDS CAN FIT ANYWHERE

Perhaps you have a sunny patch of ground available, but you don't want to go through the trouble of digging into and amending the hard-packed earth. Or maybe you rent your home, and your landlord doesn't want you digging up the yard. Gardening in a raised bed is a simple way to get the maximum yield from a small area without having to disturb the soil beneath. I like to think of a raised bed as my own personal salad bar, which can fit just about anywhere—as long as it's in full sun.

But what if the only place you have plenty of sun is your driveway? No problem. You can build a raised bed on top of concrete or asphalt. The key is to create a barrier between the impervious surface and the soil that your veggies are growing in to provide proper drainage, block contaminants, and keep your plants from cooking on the hot surface. Shovel a layer of wood chips several inches thick onto an area 2 feet wider and longer than your raised bed. Keep the chips in place by edging the area with bricks or stones. Center the box accordingly, then place a layer of cardboard along the bottom to keep the soil from washing out and to prevent asphalt oils from coming in contact with the soil. Then, fill the bed with soil that is free of weed seeds.

I used this technique last year to build one of my signature salad-bar gardens on top of a thin parking strip alongside a sidewalk (see the sidebar on the facing page). To construct the bed, I used 8-inch-wide, rot-resistant cedar planks. I avoid using pressure-treated wood because it contains chemicals that can leach into the soil. I stacked two of the boards on top of each other to create a depth of 16 inches. The deeper the bed, the more room that plants have to spread out their root systems (leading to better health) and the less watering you'll have to do. I made my box sturdy by attaching 2×2 posts to each corner.

You can make your bed as long and as wide as your space can accommodate. Mine ended up being 6 feet long and 4 feet wide. Keep in mind that the bed should be narrow enough so that you can comfortably reach into the center from either side. This allows you to tend your garden without stepping into it and compacting the soil. In this one small bed, I planted a wide array of veggies, herbs, and edible flowers—enough to make a luscious and vibrant salad for lunch or dinner on a daily basis.

And remember, containers are just another form of a raised bed. Depending on how much or how little space you've got, you can use traditional clay pots, wooden fruit crates, galvanized-steel garbage cans, or plastic buckets—anything that holds soil will work as long as you can drill holes in the bottom.

GET SUCCESS WITH INTENSIVE PLANTING

To get the biggest possible harvest from your containers and small raised beds, you need to ignore traditional spacing requirements. Don't get me wrong: I still allow room for my plants to grow, but I often take what the plant label says and cut it in half. Spacing requirements are usually based on traditional, inground gardens consisting of long, single rows spaced at least 3 feet apart so that farmers can navigate machinery up and down the rows. An intensively planted garden keeps wasted space to a minimum. Also, crops that are continually harvested—like lettuce—rarely reach their full-grown size, so they can be placed close together. Placing your plants closer to each other also crowds out weeds and protects your soil from the drying effects of the sun and wind.

At the center or rear of your container or raised bed, plant things that like to climb—such as tomatoes, cucumbers, and peas—to save space and to keep fruit off the ground. Even vines with heavy fruit, like squash or melons, can be trained upward on a bamboo tepee or railing. Use sections of panty hose or old dish towels, and make little hammocks to support the fruit as it grows.

To save even more room, sprinkle some lettuce, spinach, or arugula seeds around the base of tall edibles, like dill, fennel, peppers, and eggplant. The greens will sprout quickly and thrive in the shade produced by their taller neighbors when the weather gets hot. Creepers—like strawberries, tomatillos, thyme, and nasturtium—make good perimeter plants because they take up minimal amounts of space by cascading over the sides of containers and beds.

EMBED EDIBLES WITH ORNAMENTALS

If you're not sure you want to commit to maintaining raised beds or containerized veggies, you can incorporate edibles into the existing landscape around your home.

CREATE THE PERFECT VEGGIE PARTNERSHIP

Certain vegetables, when planted together, can help each other out. One of the most famous partnerships, called "the Three Sisters," groups beans, corn, and squash together (below). But there are numerous other beneficial partnerships in the veggie world, as well as some bad pairings to avoid.

GOOD PAIRINGS

- Asparagus and parsley. Parsley repels the dreaded asparagus beetle.
- Nasturtium and squash. Nasturtium repels squash bugs.
- Eggplant and lima beans. Lima beans deter the Colorado potato beetle, which destroys eggplants.

BAD PAIRINGS

- Tomatoes and potatoes. Both are prone to blight and often infect each other with the disease.
- Corn and tomatoes. Planting them together increases the chances of attracting the harmful tomato hornworm and corn earworm, which destroy fruit.
- Cabbage and lettuce/strawberries. Cabbage competes for the same nutrients as lettuce and strawberries.

Vegetables can be formal. Spruce up an ornamental garden with a unique focal point: an edible bean trellis.

Many edibles with notable colors, textures, or forms can be used in place of ornamentals.

Ornamental gardens often lack vertical accents. To add a tall twist to an otherwise flat garden, I like to build tepees and grow a variety of beans or peas on them (see the photo above). Many members of the legume family have not only delicious edible pods but also beautiful flowers and lush foliage. Unless your garden contains tropical foliage, you are probably in need of some plants with bold forms, as well. I like to mix in some broad-leaved squash (see the top photo on the facing page) in ornamental gardens to add impact. And when it comes to texture, I love to tuck in the puckered leaves of 'Lacinato' kale or the fuzzy fronds of artichokes. Red or rainbow chard has a cool texture as well as vibrant coloring (see the bottom photo on the facing page). My other favorite plants to use for their standout hues are 'Red Sails' lettuce and purple basil. Why plant green when you can have the same great taste with a brighter-colored option?

Remember that the blooms of many herbs last longer and are more eye-catching than many ornamentals. Onions and garlic chives (see the photo above) display globes of tiny blossoms in spring that rival any ornamental allium in beauty. Hardy herbs—such as rosemary, sage, and lavender—can easily take the place of evergreens in warm zones, whereas thyme can make a fragrant and delicious ground cover. But my favorite edible addition to existing landscapes are blueberries: Replace any deciduous shrub with a blueberry bush for beautiful fall foliage and pretty white flowers in spring; the berries are a bonus.

With so many different options, there's no reason (or excuse) not to find space for at least a few vegetables. With a bit of creativity and some effort, you can have access to fresh, mouthwatering food for much of the year—something an ornamental grass can never provide.

ABOVE Is this a bold, expensive tropical plant? Nope, it's a broad-leaved squash. It adds a unique form to this beautiful bed, while the garlic chives in back provide a delicious, long-lasting floral display.

LEFT No backyard? No problem. A tiny roadside raised bed stops traffic and provides plenty of fresh produce.

GARNISH YOUR GARDEN
WITH EDIBLES

Veggies don't have to be relegated to a separate garden. In fact, author Nancy J. Ondra argues you should choose your edibles at the same time you choose your ornamentals.

IN THE QUEST TO FIND SOMETHING NEW AND DIFFERENT FOR your garden each spring, it's easy to zoom right past the offerings of veggie seeds and transplants on your way to the glitzier displays of flower-filled annuals and perennials. Don't be too quick, though, to dismiss vegetables as merely practical plants. If you consider them purely from a design standpoint—for their interesting form, their colorful leaves, their dramatic blooms, and their showy fruit—you'll see that many vegetables easily rival more traditional ornamentals. And they have the advantage of being tasty as well as attractive.

There's nothing new, of course, about blurring the line between edible and ornamental plantings. That's a cornerstone of the traditional cottage-garden style and of a potager. It's a little different, though, to first look at vegetables for their decorative features, and then to make allowances for the possibility of picking them. The primary point here isn't raising enough food to feed your family through the winter or making dramatic design

The tall, vibrant red shoots of 'Hopi Red Dye' amaranth and 'Rubra' orach along with the purple stalk and lacy leaves of 'Redbor' kale are deliciously ornamental.

Surprise garden visitors with cabbage as your border edging. The spreading leaves mimic a hosta's outward growth, but the mounded heads provide more interest.

statements with artfully patterned vegetable plantings. It's the joy of creating exciting combinations and beautiful gardens with plants that you could pick if you have the time and desire to do so.

So what sets the best edibles apart from the rest? They're undeniably ornamental even if you never harvest from them. They may have distinctive foliage that contributes color or texture over an extended period or even through the entire growing season. They may have striking flower forms that are guaranteed to grab interest from bud stage through seed formation. Or they may produce an abundance of long-lasting fruit that take on rich colors as they ripen. And the best edibles—the pick of the crop, as it were—combine two or more of these traits in one plant.

ADD VEGGIES FOR A BOLD STATEMENT

A number of plants from the family Brassicaceae (also known as Cruciferae) have long been prized for their edible parts—specifically, in the case of cabbage, kale, and Brussels sprouts, for their nutritious foliage. But even if you don't relish the thought of eating them, these brassicas offer some absolutely stunning shapes and leaf textures, contributing height, mass, and color to ornamental combinations.

In sunny gardens, for instance, plants such as cabbage and its nonheading relatives Portuguese kale (*Brassica oleracea* var. *tronchuda*, annual) and 'Red Russian' kale (*Brassica napus pabularia* 'Red Russian', annual) fill the role that hostas (*Hosta* spp. and cvs., USDA Hardiness Zones 3–9) perform so admirably in shade gardens: providing broad mounds of large leaves to counterbalance an abundance of tiny or lacy leaves and flowers. And the bold, rounded heads of maturing cabbage stop traffic in their own right, creating a dramatic accent that's unlike anything you can get from a traditional ornamental.

Kale is another brassica that doesn't get much respect as an ornamental, but it's invaluable for its height and form. The ultimate height varies by variety, but when you plant out seedlings in spring and let them grow through the whole season, some can easily reach 3 to 4 feet tall by fall. That allows you to plant them in the middle of the border, where their broad foliage clumps can rise through the seasons as their companions mature. Placing lower, bushy plants in front of the kale gives you the option of harvesting the lower kale leaves through the summer

without leaving visible bare stems. Good choices for tall-growing kales are 'Redbor' and 'Winterbor'.

Kales offer a range of leaf textures, as well. Many are strongly crinkled or frilly on the edges; others, such as Russian types (which mature at about 18 inches tall), have flatter, jagged-edged foliage. 'Nero di Toscana' is great for foliage as well as height, with long, slender leaves that have a distinctive pebbly texture.

Brussels sprouts also will likely inspire wows in the border. Starting out as loose, low heads of broad leaves, like cabbage, they also grow upward, like some types of kale, usually to about 30 inches by the end of the growing season. By late summer, the sprouts, which resemble miniature cabbages, form at the leaf joints along the stout main stem, adding even more interest. You can surround the plants with low companions to get the full effect of a leafy topknot above the knobby stem, or you could use bushier companions and just enjoy the leafy tops as midborder accents.

Cabbage-family crops grow quickly, so you get the full effect of their ornamental qualities in just one growing season. While they are technically biennials (producing

ABOVE Which plants aren't the ornamentals? 'Redbor' kale and 'Bright Lights' chard look right at home with black-eyed Susans.

RIGHT It's an eye grabber. Brussels sprouts make an ornamental impact as well as any bold-leaved tropical.

'Hopi Red Dye' amaranth adds back-of-the-border bang with its red-burgundy color that follows the theme of the area.

To create a bold focal point, the eye-catching foliage comes from Portuguese kale, not from an exotic ornamental.

For front-of-the-border color, this purple basil provides a color punch that won't quit.

STAY ON TOP OF FOLIAGE PESTS

One of the biggest problems for plants in the cabbage family is caterpillars, who chew large holes in the leaves. Many times, the problem is minor, and you can deal with it by handpicking the pests or snipping off affected leaves; spraying with the biological control agent Bt (*Bacillus thuringiensis* var. *kurstaki*) greatly minimizes the damage. The holes that flea beetles create in the leaves of mustard, bok choy, and eggplant are tinier, but their damage is equally unattractive. They can be difficult to control, but sprays based on spinosad, neem, or capsaicin may help.

flowers and seeds the following year), it's best to treat them as annuals, harvesting the usable parts when you do fall cleanup or removing the plants in fall or early spring, then replanting.

If you'd prefer something big and bold without the bother of yearly replanting, then look beyond the cabbage family to some handsome perennial vegetables. In mild climates, artichokes (*Cynara scolymus* and cvs., Zones 8–9) are fantastic as foliage accents, with large, jagged-edged, gray-green to silvery leaves in dense clumps that can easily fill a space 3 to 4 feet across. The plants send up branching stems in summer, with gigantic buds that open into amazing thistlelike, electric blue flowers if you don't pick them.

In cooler regions, consider rhubarb (*Rheum rhabarbarum* and cvs., Zones 3–9) instead. Give it a site with compost-enriched soil, and in a few years, you'll enjoy a splendid show of broad, red-stemmed, bright green leaves in a clump 2 to 3 feet tall and 3 to 4 feet wide. Left alone, mature clumps send up 3-foot-tall stalks that carry plumes of white flowers in summer. Rhubarb might go dormant during the hottest part of summer, unless you plan to mulch heavily and water regularly during dry spells. When temperatures moderate a bit and rainfall is more regular, the clumps will quickly produce fresh leaves and look great until frost. The edible part of rhubarb is its leaf stalks, not the leaves themselves. You can take generous harvests—mostly from early spring to early summer—from clumps that are at least a few years old without interfering with their ornamental value.

ADD COLOR AS WELL AS TASTE

Form and texture aren't the only contributions that vegetable plants make to the ornamental garden: They can provide outstanding color, as well.

Wonderful shapes and colors abound among the lettuces, from the bright chartreuse of 'Australian Yellow' and 'Gold Rush' to the red-speckled green of 'Flashy Trout's Back' (also known as 'Forellenschluss') to the velvety deep red of 'Merlot' and 'Outredgeous'. Beets, too, offer some outstanding dark-leaved varieties, such as 'Bull's Blood' and 'Macgregor's Favorite'. Other ornamental-and-edible options include the ferny-leaved mustards—'Golden Streaks', with yellowish green leaves, and 'Ruby Streaks', with purple leaves—and the broad-leaved bok choy variety 'Violetta', with glossy, near-black foliage.

At the other end of the height spectrum are tall edibles such as orach (*Atriplex hortensis* and cvs., annual), which can reach up to 6 feet tall. 'Golden' orach is greenish yellow; 'Rubra' orach has deep red stems, leaves, and seed heads. Another tall selection for intensely deep red stems, leaves, and seed plumes is 'Hopi Red Dye' amaranth (*Amaranthus cruentus* 'Hopi Red Dye', annual). Both the orachs and the amaranth can provide an ample supply of young leaves for salads without interfering with their border display.

Yet another must-have is Swiss chard. It grows in 1- to 2-foot-tall, fountain-shaped clumps, with bright green or deep red leaves that have contrasting veins and stalks. You can find some single-color strains, such as 'Rhubarb' and 'Charlotte' in red; 'Bright Yellow' in yellow; and 'Fordhook Giant' with bright white stems and veins. But if you really want to make the most of the color range, buy a pack of 'Bright Lights' or 'Five Color' seeds or transplants and select some of each color that appears; a mix usually includes red, orange, yellow, pink, and white.

Showy fruit are the forte of many members of the family Solanaceae, including tomatoes and peppers. Small-fruited cherry tomatoes, as well as the even tinier-fruited currant types, can climb through tuteurs or other decorative supports or scramble up through the stems of shrubby companions, festooning them with small yellow flowers and clusters of red, orange, or yellow rounded or pear-shaped fruit. Tomato plants themselves usually aren't that interesting, but for something really different, seek out 'Variegated', with cream- to white-splashed leaves and medium-size red fruit.

Peppers form low, bushy plants in the range of 1 to 3 feet tall. Their fruits are usually green or deep purple when they first form, ripening to bright shades of red, orange, yellow, or purple, and they range in size and shape from tiny round globes or tapering cones to substantial, blocky, bell-type peppers. Those with the most abundant, most colorful, and most easily visible fruit are the scorchingly hot types, such as the exquisite 'Black Pearl', which also offers deep purple foliage. You can also find, however, equally ornamental selections with easier-to-eat fruit, such as multicolored 'Sweet Pickles'.

Why waste space on plants that are just pretty faces? If you start mixing in some that are both showy and productive, you'll never be at a loss for a side dish or salad fixings.

This colorful combination tastes good, too. Pair 'Black Pearl' pepper with 'Australian Yellow' lettuce.

FRONT-YARD BEAUTY

Don't be afraid to put your vegetable garden front and center. With a few simple design tips from garden designer Darcy Daniels, you'll be proud to put your edibles on display.

IT SEEMS LIKE EVERYONE WANTS TO GROW VEGETABLES THESE days, but many homeowners are reluctant to do so in their front yard, even when it happens to be the sunniest, most desirable spot. After all, vegetable gardens can get chaotic by the end of the growing season, and they tend to look stark and bare in the off-season. Front-yard veggie gardens, though, can be created that have multiseasonal appeal, such as the garden that I designed for Kristan and Ben Sias in Portland, Oregon. Kristan, an avid cook, had been growing edibles in a small, out-of-the-way corner of her front yard for years. The location's size and limited sunlight prevented her from growing the amount and variety of food that she wanted. This new design and location, however, offers plenty of room for edibles—plus, a pleasing street-side view.

Easy access is just one of the perks that this front-yard veggie garden has to offer. The side door to the right of the garage leads straight to the kitchen, making it a short commute from garden to table.

LET THE SPACE INSPIRE THE DESIGN

A front-yard vegetable garden requires as much attention and forethought as a highly visible ornamental garden, especially when space is at a premium. Start planning your layout by considering the shape of your space; employ curves, angles, and straight lines to create an efficient and artful design.

The layout of the Siases' vegetable garden works with the shape of their driveway, which curves along the upper portion. A 20-foot-wide section of yard is available in the front, tapering to a narrow 6½-foot-wide strip at the rear. A mix of straight lines and curves makes the most of this unique space (see the sidebar below). The raised beds are laid out in a grid of 5-foot squares modified with curves, resulting in a geometric pattern with pleasing and practical proportions that ground the garden. The geometric grid also instills a sense of order and visual appeal when the garden is overflowing with produce, as well as when it's

THREE STEPS TRANSFORM A BLANK SLATE INTO A DREAM GARDEN

Moving your veggie garden from the background to the foreground takes some effort. A permanent raised-bed design for a front-yard location requires more planning the first time around than an annual backyard veggie garden. This extra effort and forethought pays off in the long run, requiring less labor in the years to come. Follow these three steps to help transform your available front-yard space into an amazing edible garden.

1. PLAN THE LAYOUT.

Consider a number of options before landing on a final design. Brainstorm with tissue overlays on a base map—this lets you quickly and freely rough out choices. Once an idea resonates, firm up the preferred concept by fine-tuning the dimensions and determining construction details. Keep in mind that the human eye is able to pick up remarkably small deviations in alignment. Geometric patterns require a bit more rigid planning and a deeper understanding of your site than nongeometric ones.

2. SHAPE THE BEDS.

If you decide to incorporate tight curves in your design, you will need to have a fabricator roll (shape) the steel. Don't be dissuaded by this extra step. Steel shapes can be mathematically described and then fabricated in a straightforward process, which shouldn't break the bank if you keep your design relatively simple.

3. CHOOSE THE PLANTS.

Edibles that will be on display in your front yard should bring more to the table than just good eating. Think foliage, flowers, and fruit. Attractive foliage is readily available in plants such as kale, rhubarb, artichoke, chard, and lettuce. The flowers of nasturtiums, scarlet runner beans, and espaliered apples provide colorful blooms, while fruits such as 'Sun Gold' tomatoes, eggplant, peppers (especially red ones), and blueberries provide additional interest.

BEFORE

AFTER

dormant. An additional interior curve in the central garden space not only lends artistic flair but also enlarges the central intersection, which would otherwise be too narrow and awkward to maneuver within.

When designing a garden layout, plan for adequate pathways and points of access so that you have room to work in the garden. Keep your main pathway at least 3 feet wide to maneuver within—supplemental pathways can be narrower yet still serviceable. Raised beds wider than 4 feet are difficult to work in, but incorporating enough usable pathways to provide access from multiple sides makes tending and harvesting easier.

PICK MATERIALS FOR STYLE AND FUNCTION

Regardless of whether you have inground beds or raised beds, use attractive weatherproof materials to define them. The Siases' garden uses a great material: steel. It is low maintenance, lasts indefinitely, and is space efficient. I also like the warm, earthy tones of rusted steel. The flat-bar steel used in the Siases' garden is only $3/16$ inch thick, making it easy to shape. This allows the design to steer away from straight lines toward graceful curves and more complex geometric shapes. You can opt to create the beds yourself, but because of the complex layout employed in this design, the Siases hired a local contractor to make and install the steel frames. The do-it-yourself route will require you to locate a local industrial-materials supplier or metal fabricator, which may be easier to find if you're located near a major city. You'll also want to call ahead to make sure that the company doesn't operate strictly as a wholesale supplier.

Although steel is great, other materials can be used successfully, too. Cedar and composite lumber work well for beds that utilize straight lines and regular angles. Brick or natural stone can be used to create long-lasting edging that feels organic. A hedge of dwarf boxwood can serve as a living evergreen boundary if you're not using raised beds and are willing to put in a bit more labor to maintain it. Remember, however, to take the thickness of your edging material into consideration. Natural stone or a planted edge will be tricky for small beds because they'll take up a greater percentage of your growing area. With the raised-bed or border material chosen, pathway materials come next. The paths of the Siases' garden use compacted gravel to provide all-season access and to achieve a neat, crisp appearance that's especially attractive next to the warm tones of rusted metal. The gravel, the steel, and the adjacent driveway all have a tendency to capture and radiate heat, a boon when growing heat-loving veggies, such as tomatoes or peppers.

ADD ORNAMENTS THAT HAVE A PURPOSE

Trellises, decorative cages, and garden ornaments provide the finishing touch to a garden. The open central axis of the Siases' garden incorporates a focal point to add interest to the space both during and after the growing season. The Siases commissioned an art-glass piece by two local artists (see the photo on p. 18). The glass underscores the garden's unified color theme (created by the combination of materials, structures, and ornaments), which helps ensure that all the details in the garden come together as a whole. A similar artistic display can be achieved in your own garden by incorporating a unifying central focal point, such as a pot, birdbath, fountain, or other decorative element.

Working ornamentation, like trellises and cages, saves space and gives your plants support—but it need not be ordinary or an eyesore. The Siases' garden uses circular tomato cages made by a local artisan; the cages' rusted-steel texture blends perfectly with the edging of the beds.

Aesthetics aside, most support structures need to be easy to move from bed to bed. While the layout and position of your beds are constant, the types of plants grown in them will vary from year to year as you rotate your crops.

Many plants will grow on a structure where they're encouraged to twine and climb. The Siases' espaliered apples along their boundary fence are a decorative and space-saving way to incorporate fruit. Because space is tight in many city gardens, growing vertically provides extra room, and the varying heights bring added visual interest to the garden.

Be careful, though, not to overdo it. Too much ornamentation can create chaos and visual clutter. The cohesiveness of the Siases' garden can be at least partly attributed to a disciplined color palette and limited materials. Choose similar themes and stick to them. The results will give you almost as much pleasure as eating your own homegrown fruits and vegetables.

EASY & EDIBLE
PLANTING DESIGNS

Beds full of edibles look just as good as your flower gardens, except you can eat what's planted in them. Take your pick from Seed Savers Exchange's cofounder Diane Ott Whealy's garden plans—or try them all!

I CONSIDER MYSELF PRETTY LUCKY TO HAVE THOUSANDS OF heirloom vegetable, flower, and herb varieties in my backyard—which happens to be Seed Savers Exchange's Heritage Farm in Decorah, Iowa. Although beautiful in their own right, these fields of edibles aren't exactly picturesque because they are planted for the sole purpose of harvesting and preserving seed. To better showcase the beauty of edibles, we decided to transform an area next to our barn into a productive—yet good-looking—garden plot. Visitors love the new gardens so much that they often ask us how they can create similar plantings.

Anyone can have edible gardens that look as good as they taste. I've blended more than 250 different plant types in this one space, all serving ornamental and practical purposes. While I don't expect anyone to go that far, the following are some of my favorite raised-bed planting plans, which use some of the most attractive edibles available.

An entire garden of edibles can be beautiful as well as delicious. Different sizes and shapes for the beds add interest.

POPPING CORN AT THE CENTER

Direct-sow 'Tom Thumb' popcorn 10 inches apart in
a block in the middle of a 3-foot-square raised bed.
Fill in around the corn and to the edge of the box with
nasturtiums. Space those seeds 1 foot apart. For a
different color scheme, use 'Strawberry' popcorn instead
of 'Tom Thumb' and mix in strawberry spinach, a self-
seeding annual, with the nasturtium. The spinach is
showy and has nutritious triangular leaves, which can be
steamed or used in salads; its red fruit is edible, too. The
popcorn adds a vertical focal point, while the beautiful
(and edible) nasturtiums and spinach make productive
use of the thin perimeter.

1 'Tom Thumb' or 'Strawberry' popcorn

2 Nasturtium (*Tropaeolum* spp. and cvs., annual)

3 Strawberry spinach (*Chenopodium capitatum*, annual)

A 3-foot-square raised bed

A rectangular raised bed,
13 feet long and 3 feet
wide. Set chicken wire
down the center in the
shape of an S curve,
securing it on either end
with a sturdy wooden stake.

1 'Blue Podded' shelling
peas

2 Wild celery (*Apium
graveolens*, Zones 8–9)

3 Lettuce, assorted mix of
colors

4 'Bishop's Children'
dahlia (Zones 9–11)*

5 'Prizetaker' leek

6 Sweet alyssum
(*Lobularia maritima*,
annual)*

* Nonedible plants

PEAS PLANTED ON A CURVE

Direct-sow the 'Blue Podded' shelling peas along the
bottom of the chicken-wire trellis, spaced 2 to 4 inches
apart. Plant wild celery in a rectangle, 1 foot away from
the trellis and spaced 8 inches apart. Between the celery,
alternate planting the lettuces and dahlias—lettuces
between one pair of celery and dahlias between another.
This gives the entire bed a color-block appearance, which
is stunning. Randomly plant the leeks throughout the
bed; as they grow taller, they will end up looking like giant
fireworks exploding from the foliage below. Complete the
design with low growers, like sweet alyssum, placed at
the very edges of the bed and poking out from underneath
the lettuce leaves.

FOOD AND FLOWERS

Direct-sow the 'Scarlet' runner beans 6 inches apart at the base of the tepee so that they'll be able to climb it. This structure provides a focal point in an edible bed while serving as a sturdy support for the rambunctious runner beans. Working 1 foot out from the tepee, direct-sow the 'Bull's Blood' beets in a circle; the seeds should be spaced 3 inches apart. Beets are just as pretty as any ornamental-foliage plant, and they tolerate a wide range of soils without complaint. Another 6 inches out from the beets, transplant African daisies, spaced 1 foot apart, around the outer circle of beets. Between the African daises, plant a couple of 'Spicy Globe' basils (which stay nice and compact) and a couple of ornamental peppers. Plant low growers, like moss rose, sensitive plant, and sweet alyssum, so that they spill over the very edges of the octagon, softening its sides.

1 'Scarlet' runner bean

2 'Bull's Blood' beet

3 African daisy (*Osteospermum* spp. and cvs., annual)*

4 'Spicy Globe' basil

5 Ornamental pepper

6 Moss rose (*Portulaca grandiflora* cvs., annual)*

7 Sensitive plant (*Mimosa pudica*, Zones 12–13)*

8 Sweet alyssum*

*Nonedible plants

THREE BIG FLAVORS

Set out the 'Red Russian' or 'Lacinato' kale as soon as the soil can be worked in spring. Choose only one variety (don't mix them), because it makes a greater impact visually when all of one kind is massed together. Plant three to five kale plants (spaced 7 inches apart) at the center of the bed. Working out 1 foot from the kales, fill the box with parsley, spaced 6 inches apart. Place one 'Red Marietta' marigold in each corner of the bed. The fine texture of the parsley and marigolds help the puckered-skinned kales shine as the focal point in this bed.

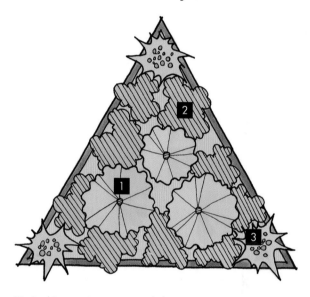

1 'Red Russian' or 'Lacinato' kale

2 'Triple Curled' or Italian flat-leaf parsley

3 'Red Marietta' marigold (*Tagetes patula* 'Red Marietta', annual)

A triangular raised bed, 5 feet long on each side

ROOT

LEGUME

FRUIT

LEAF

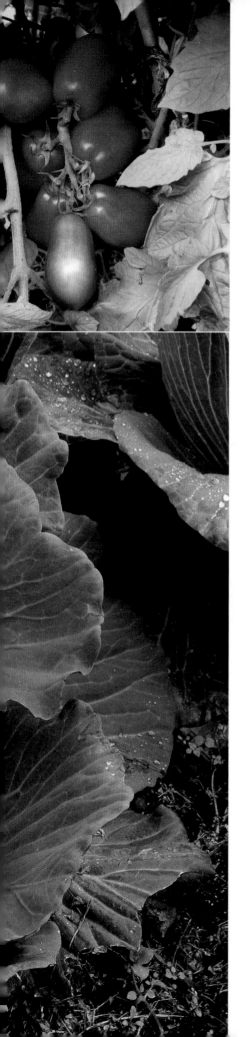

CROP ROTATION
FOR ANY GARDEN

Crop rotation might seem out of reach if you have a small space, but it's not. All you need to do is divide your space into four areas—you decide how big—and follow gardener Cynthia Hizer's advice for success.

WHERE DID I PUT THE ARUGULA TWO YEARS AGO? AND LAST YEAR, it seems that the tomatoes were in the main garden. Or were they by the rabbit hutch? I guess I can't plant potatoes there this year—I think. If, like me, you're not keeping track of these details, you may not be getting the most out of your garden or giving your vegetables all they need. And you may be making needless work for yourself.

Moving plants around from year to year is one of the best organic techniques to minimize disease and bug problems and to maximize soil fertility. Various rotation plans are popular. The simplest is "don't plant the same thing in the same place two years in a row." This strategy is designed to ward off pests. If the cabbage looper pupa nestles down in the cabbage debris in October and reawakens the following spring to more cabbage, that's instant sustenance. But if you've moved the cabbage, the looper may die trying to find its food.

Some gardeners move plants around by family: nightshade, brassica, and cucurbit, for example. For this system, it's helpful to have a working knowledge of Latin as well as an intimate knowledge of plant parts. One well-known gardening expert

FROM LEFT TO RIGHT Leaf crops use nitrogen. Fruit crops use phosphorus. Root crops use potassium.

suggests a 10-year rotation. But I get dizzy just thinking of the complications. What if I sell the house before 10 years are up? Should the rotation plan be in my will?

I use a system that's easy to implement and easy to remember without a notebook. I separate my crops based on their nutritional requirements. It so happens that the plants fall pretty neatly into leafy crops, fruiting crops, and root crops. A fourth division is for legumes—peas and beans—which technically are fruits, but they get their own plot because they actually add more nutrients to the soil than they take. By default, this system separates families and thus helps diminish pest problems. Leaf, fruit, root, legume—that's my crop-rotation plan. No detailed plant anatomy, no bookkeeping, and no Latin (which I still plan to learn someday).

TEST THE SOIL, THEN AMEND

I started by having my soil tested at a lab. I then added the recommended nutrients—manure, compost, black rock phosphate, greensand, gypsum, and lime—to my entire garden. I did this in fall so that the amendments would have time to break down and become available to the plants.

In spring, I divided the garden into four sections and planted each with one of the groups: leaf, fruit, root, or legume. Every year, I now rotate the plantings so that the leaf group moves to where the legumes grew the season before, and the other groups all move over a section.

Legumes add nitrogen.

Having four areas of roughly equal size makes this system work, even though you'll probably want to grow more of one kind of crop than another. I made each division big enough to hold the largest group that I grow, and I fill the empty spaces in my less-crowded sections with cover crops. If the areas aren't the same size, you'll be tempted, when it comes time to put the largest group— say, the fruits—into a too-small space, to sneak some extra tomatoes or peppers into an area where they don't belong. And then your system will have been breached.

Another benefit to this rotation system is that it's easy to remember when and where to add soil amendments. Every fall, I amend only the bed that will hold next year's leaf crop. First, I get my soil tested, then I add manure and whatever amendments the test results recommend—lime, rock phosphate, greensand. At this time, I also spread compost over the entire garden. This program is based on using organic amendments, which stay in the soil longer than nonorganic fertilizers. If you're not using cover crops, you'll need to add manure to each bed every year.

BED 1: LEAF CROPS

Leaves love nitrogen, so the plants in this group need plenty of nitrogen to build strong stems and leaves. Nitrogen is the most readily soluble of all the nutrients and, therefore, the hardest for the soil to hold on to. So it's important to grow leaf crops in soil that's had a fresh infusion of nitrogen. Manure or a cover crop is the cornerstone. During the growing season, I also give the plants in the leaf bed some extra amendments (fish or blood meal). Leaf crops include lettuce, herbs, cabbage, kale, broccoli, cauliflower, and spinach.

BED 2: FRUIT CROPS

Everything that develops as a result of a flower being pollinated is a fruit. And for fruit, phosphorus is a must. These crops need a generous amount of phosphorus to set blossoms and to develop fruit. If the soil is rich in nitrogen, the leaves will be luxurious, but flowers and fruit will be few. Bonemeal and rock phosphate are the best sources of phosphorus to add to your soil. Bonemeal breaks down sooner than rock phosphate and needs to be renewed more often. Rock phosphate is my favorite; it takes a year to become fully available, but one application lasts five years. Fruit crops include tomatoes, cucumbers, squash, peppers, and eggplant.

BED 3: ROOT CROPS

Roots rely mainly on potassium. At the same time, they need even less nitrogen than fruit. That's fine because, by the third year of my rotation plan, most of the nitrogen has been used up in a given bed, but the leisurely potassium is ready and waiting to go to work. If I need to add potassium, my favorite source is greensand, because it also yields dozens of trace minerals and helps break up clay soil. Wood ashes, gypsum, kelp, and granite dust

are also good sources of potassium. Root crops include radishes, carrots, turnips, beets, onions, and leeks.

BED 4: LEGUME CROPS

Legumes put nitrogen back into the soil. Beans and peas pull nitrogen from the air and store it on their roots. I grow these in the last bed of the cycle because when their roots decompose in the soil, the nitrogen becomes available for the following year's leaf crop. The spent plants, when turned into the garden, add organic matter. Legume crops include peas and beans.

EVERY RULE HAS ITS EXCEPTIONS

I've had a hard time deciding where to put corn, potatoes, and garlic, but I'm happy with what I'm doing now. Corn is a heavy user of nitrogen, so I grow it in the leaf rotation, even though corn is a fruiting crop. In fact, I plant corn seed right into my lettuce patch; the growing corn shades the lettuce and takes over when the lettuce is finished.

Potatoes are roots, but they are also in the nightshade family, which includes tomatoes, peppers, and eggplants. I noticed that the potatoes suffered more pest problems when they followed their relatives. I now plant potatoes in the legume bed, which keeps them two years away from their kin.

And, finally, garlic is a little awkward because its growing season stretches from fall to summer. I now plant garlic in October in the fruit bed, which will be the root bed the following year.

ROTATE THE CROPS!

Because these four crop types need different nutrients from the soil, the key to proper growth is rotation. During the next growing season, Bed 1 replaces Bed 4, Bed 2 replaces Bed 1, Bed 3 replaces Bed 2, and Bed 4 replaces Bed 3. As long as you cycle your beds properly, your plants will thrive.

BUILDING BETTER SOIL

Healthy soil means healthier plants and a bountiful harvest, so don't shortchange the prep work. Gardener Joe Queirolo shares his three-step, natural approach to high-quality soil.

A BACKYARD IS NO PLACE FOR A FARM. MY EARLIEST VEGETABLE gardens were small-scale imitations of large-scale farms. I rototilled the soil, spread bagged chemical fertilizer all around, and built neat hills and straight furrows. I worked like a tractor. Then I unleashed a flood of water to fill the furrows and bring life to the land. I engineered like a god. Months later, I would make my daily rounds to harvest what I could from the hard, gray soil that was cracking under the intense summer sun. Farming was a tough life.

Did it have to be so tough? In reading about vegetable growing, I discovered that it did not.

The key to successful gardening is taking good care of the soil. By deeply cultivating the soil and adding plenty of organic matter and natural fertilizers, I not only increased the production of my garden many times over but also entered into a new relationship with my soil. I tended it and nurtured it, and my backyard farm gradually became a garden.

Good soil leads to robust plants. Because plants tend to be healthier and more productive when grown in well-prepared soil, you make the best use of your garden space.

LEFT Loosen the soil for stronger roots. By thrusting a digging fork as deep as you can, then working it back and forth, you'll allow roots to penetrate the soil more easily.

ABOVE Vibrant soil beats lifeless clay. The soil on the left is well tended and full of life, a far cry from the clay soil on the right, which would be nearly impossible to garden with.

DIG THE SOIL, DON'T TURN IT OVER

If you're making a new bed in unbroken ground, use a spading shovel to cut the edges. Then loosen the ground with a digging fork, thrusting it as deep into the soil as you can. Rock the handle back to loosen and lift the soil, but try not to turn it over. Remember that soil is a vibrant ecosystem that suffers if it's exposed to too much light and air. So just wiggle the fork around to make it easier for roots to penetrate. Deep cultivation will encourage the roots to grow downward. If you can dig your bed only 6 to 8 inches deep the first year, don't worry. Earthworms and plant roots will penetrate even farther, loosening the soil so that you can dig a little deeper the following year.

I don't use a rototiller to loosen the soil. Excessive mechanical tilling can destroy organic matter by over-aerating the soil. It can also create a layer of compacted soil in the subsoil just below the depth where the blades reach. Roots will have a tough time growing down into such hard soil. Besides, tillers are noisy, smoky, and tricky to maneuver in small spaces.

Break up soil clumps, and rake out the grass. Use a cultivator or a rake to work over the bed, giving it a rough shape, breaking up clumps of soil and pulling out grass as you go. For this task, I rely on a cultivator I've had for years; in fact, once I've completed the initial groundbreaking with a digging fork, I can do almost everything else with my cultivator.

You'll need to loosen the soil and break up clumps each year in preparation for planting, but it won't take as much effort as it will the first year.

FEED THE SOIL WITH ORGANIC MATTER

The bacteria, fungi, actinomycetes, and other organisms that inhabit your soil will convert the food that you give them (compost, manure, organic fertilizers, or plant residues) into nutrients for your growing plants. As they release nutrients, these organisms are also creating humus (minuscule particles of decomposed organic matter) and binding soil particles into irregular clumps. Over time, the regular addition of organic matter will improve the structure of your soil. This will help sandy soil hold water and nutrients longer and will help clay soil drain faster and allow roots to penetrate it more easily.

The first time I prepare a bed, I add at least 3 inches of compost. That works out to about 1 cubic yard for every 100 square feet. You can use homemade compost, livestock manure, commercial compost, or mushroom compost—whatever may be cheap, abundant, and available. Because this initial amending is large, it pays to shop around for a material that you can get in bulk rather than in bags. I would avoid sawdust. The high carbon content of wood products tends to reduce the availability of nitrogen in the soil.

I rake the manure out evenly over the bed and cut it into the top 3 to 4 inches of soil, using either a cultivator or a fork. If you use a digging fork, stir in the compost with a twisting motion. If you find it awkward to reach to the center of the bed with a fork, lay a board across the bed to give you a place to stand without compacting the soil. Finally, I use my rake to blend the manure in evenly and shape the bed surface.

In the following seasons, you will need to add only an inch or two of organic matter. Remember, however, that no two years are alike—in weather conditions or in the crops you choose to grow. So be adaptable, and pay close attention to your soil. If it begins to lose its crumbly structure or gets hard or sticky, you can add organic matter in spring and again in fall. A warm summer combined with moderate watering and intensive planting can use up organic matter quickly.

DON'T FORGET THE FERTILIZER

Organic matter is essential for the smooth functioning of soil life. But when you are growing vegetables, you cannot rely on organic matter alone to supply all of the necessary nutrients. Plants need plenty of nitrogen, phosphorus, and potassium (the N-P-K on a fertilizer bag) and lesser amounts of nutrients such as copper, magnesium, boron, and iron (the so-called trace minerals or micronutrients).

Manure from cows, horses, or other herbivores and a compost of decomposed plant material will contain most of the trace minerals your soil needs. Most soils already have adequate phosphorus and potassium. Nitrogen's most important role is to promote vegetative tissue (leaves and stems), so it's essential for healthy plant growth. And it is soluble, which means that it can be washed out of the root zone, away from your plants. So nitrogen needs to be renewed regularly.

I use organic sources of nitrogen to feed the soil, not chemical fertilizers to feed the plant. Organic materials have to be digested by soil microorganisms in order to release nutrients. This slower process is dependent on soil temperature, moisture, and the size, density, and composition of the organic material. The biological activity you encourage by using natural materials will improve your soil, which, in turn, will lead to healthier plants.

I use fish meal (dried and pulverized fish waste) to supply my growing plants with nitrogen. It's available from mail-order, farm-supply, and garden-supply companies. If you want a more available organic source of nitrogen, you can use dried blood meal. It's less expensive than fish meal but doesn't supply quite as wide a range of nutrients.

Here in the West, nitrogen is generally in short supply, so my standard dosage is ½ pound per 100 square feet. Your soil might not need quite as much nitrogen as mine does. To know for sure, you'd have to have it tested by a soil lab. But most gardeners can probably safely apply ½ pound of nitrogen per 100 square feet as long as it's a slow-release organic fertilizer.

I broadcast the fish meal over the bed and chop it in with a rake. I'm careful not to rake it in because I want it to stay evenly distributed. Because our summers are dry, I then use the back of the rake to smooth the surface flat so that the bed will catch all the water I put on it.

Now the soil is loosened and amended. The beds are shaped and fertilized. The microorganisms are ready to go to work for you as soon as you add water and plants. Just remember that you are creating more than just a garden. You are managing a simplified ecosystem. Learn to work with nature. Strive to create the conditions that allow for healthy growth. You'll get more from your garden than you ever expected.

RIGHT Organic fertilizer releases its nutrients gradually over the entire season. For the best results, broadcast the fertilizer for even distribution. To keep the fertilizer evenly distributed, chop it in with the tines of a soil rake.

2

TOMATOES

HEIRLOOM TOMATOES

Unequalled taste has kept these old-time favorites around for decades. Cook and gardener Ruth Lively helps you choose the best varieties and teaches you how to save seeds so you can grow them every year.

WORD OF MOUTH IS ALWAYS A GREAT ADVERTISEMENT. I FIRST ventured into heirloom tomatoes after hearing for the umpteenth time how swell 'Brandywine' was. If gardeners from New Jersey to California were extolling its virtues, then, I thought, it must be worth growing. And it was. Since that first 'Brandywine', I've grown 'Persimmon', 'Old Flame', 'Georgia Streak', and 'German', among others. And while I'd rather fight than give up my favorite hybrids, heirlooms now make up the lion's share of my tomato crop.

Grow the best-tasting tomatoes in town. The flavor of heirloom varieties might mean that you'll never want to plant hybrids again.

TOP LEFT 'Anna Russian': mildly sweet flavor with a nice tang

ABOVE 'Evergreen': juicy with a citrus flavor

TOP RIGHT 'Azoychka': sweet flavor with a hint of lemon

RIGHT 'Black Krim': soft flesh with an appealing, smoky flavor

FLAVOR MAKES THEM SPECIAL

Most of us cut our gardener's teeth on hybrid tomatoes, those with names like 'Jet Star' or 'Better Boy'. With few exceptions, our chosen varieties were red, round, and—for the most part—big. The bigger, the better. There's always been another side to the tomato world, though, a side where the fruits of the vine can be fluted, scalloped, flattened, lobed, or shaped like hearts or strawberries. When ripe, they might be white, pink, red, orange, yellow, gold, purple, chocolate brown, blackish red, green, or

striped. In addition to the typical tomato foliage, there are potato-leaf types; wispy, fernlike leaves; and puckered, rugose leaves. And the flavors range from sweet to tart, mild to strong, and perfumed and fruity to dark and smoky.

Part of an heirloom's charm is its history, which is often as colorful as its skin. What homeowner can resist 'Radiator Charlie's Mortgage Lifter' (see the top photo on p. 40)? This gigantic tomato was developed in the 1930s by Marshall "Radiator Charlie" Byles, who owned a radiator repair shop in West Virginia. Byles repeatedly

KNOW THE GROWTH HABITS OF YOUR TOMATOES

INDETERMINATE tomato plants continue to grow, limited only by the length of the season. These plants produce stems, leaves, and fruit as long as they live. These tomatoes will need to be pruned and staked.

DETERMINATE tomato plants have a predetermined number of stems, leaves, and flowers hardwired into their genetic structure. During the first stage of growth, all of the stems, most of the leaves, and a few fruits are formed. This is followed by a flush of flowering and a few final leaves. Finally, there is no further vegetative growth; as the tomato fruit ripens, the leaves die. No pruning or staking is needed.

SEMIDETERMINATE tomato plants, as the name implies, are somewhere between indeterminate and determinate types. Although there aren't many semideterminate tomatoes, one of the most popular hybrids, 'Celebrity', falls into this category. These might need pruning or staking.

crossed four of the biggest tomatoes he could find. When he had a stable variety, he sold transplants for a dollar apiece and, in six years, was able to pay off his mortgage.

Or take 'Cherokee Purple' (see the photo on p. 41), which dates to before 1890. About 20 years ago, Craig LeHoullier, a North Carolina chemist, got a letter and some tomato seeds from a stranger. This "purple" tomato had been in a neighbor's family for years. The stranger knew of LeHoullier's interest in heirlooms and thought that these seeds were worth trying. Most so-called purple

tomatoes are actually pink, so LeHoullier was delighted to discover this one was truly purple—and delicious, too.

Ask anybody who pledges allegiance to heirloom tomatoes the question "Why?" and chances are you'll get the same response: flavor. Heirlooms generally have more flavor than hybrids. And when you find the ones you really love, you'll be able to taste them in your dreams. Some get into heirlooms looking for tomatoes that taste like the ones our parents grew. But it isn't nostalgia that makes heirlooms taste better. It's chemistry. Most are indeterminate, meaning that they

ABOVE 'Radiator Charlie's Mortgage Lifter': marbled flesh with a well-balanced flavor

RIGHT 'Kellogg's Breakfast': dense, meaty flesh with a rich flavor

FAR RIGHT 'Cherokee Purple': extremely sweet, meaty flesh

keep putting on new growth until they die. The more foliage a plant has in relation to fruit, the better the flavor. because leaves manufacture the sugars and acids that end up in the fruit. An abundance of leaves means an abundance of sugars and acids.

There are thousands of open-pollinated tomato varieties listed in the Seed Savers Exchange yearbook. According to cofounder Kent Whealy, only a quarter of those are true heirlooms, but that still leaves us plenty to choose from. So with space for only a handful, how do you pick a winner? Probably the best way to find tomatoes worth growing is to taste them first. Sampling a recently picked, locally grown tomato will give you the best insight into whether that variety should be on your seed list.

Thanks to heirlooms' popularity, it's getting easier to find opportunities to do this. At farmers' markets, vendors may offer samplings, and organized tomato tastings are becoming standard end-of-summer events.

OLDER ISN'T ALWAYS BETTER

Just because a tomato has been around for longer than you doesn't guarantee it's going to taste great. There are duds among heirlooms, and part of that may be due to location. Heirlooms, after all, are regional—even local—varieties. A tomato cultivated for generations in eastern Pennsylvania isn't necessarily going to do well or taste great if grown in areas along the Texas coast.

Heirloom tomatoes have characteristics some people might consider disadvantages. The fruits are generally thinner skinned and softer than those of hybrids, so they're more liable to crack or bruise. That makes sense because heirlooms were selected for home gardens, rather than for commercial production. The many indeterminate varieties also need lots of staking and tying. Their exuberant growth could overwhelm the unsuspecting gardener. You can prune indeterminate tomatoes (see the illustration on p. 43). This practice reduces weight and allows more sun in to ripen the fruit, but it's also bound to sacrifice some flavor along with the loss of all those leaves.

Many heirlooms don't yield as much as hybrids, but that's partly why they have better flavor, because lower-

WHEN IS AN OLD TOMATO NOT AN HEIRLOOM?

In the broadest picture, tomatoes fall into two categories: hybrid and open-pollinated (heirlooms are a subset of the open-pollinated type).

Hybrids result from crossing two distinct parents, and they produce fruit that is different from either parent. Hybridizing tomatoes involves a lot of work. Tomato flowers contain both male and female parts; most of the time, they pollinate themselves as they open. The first step in creating a hybrid is to trim away the male parts of a flower before the pollen becomes viable, leaving behind a flower with just female parts; the pollen from the male parent is then administered. It's tedious, expensive work, which partly accounts for the high cost of hybrid seed.

Open-pollinated tomatoes were once hybrids that have been genetically stabilized by someone patiently selecting desirable fruit and growing out generations of tomatoes. Stabilizing usually takes several years, sometimes more than a dozen. Once a variety is stabilized, it will come true to seed. That is, the plants and their fruit will be the same from year to year, unless you allow your plants to cross accidentally. Thanks to tomatoes' self-pollinating nature, the odds are against that.

Heirlooms are a subset of the open-pollinated category. Most experts agree that heirlooms are open-pollinated varieties that have been in existence for at least 50 years. Some devotees have an even stricter definition: To qualify as an heirloom, it has to have been handed down through a family or a community. For these folks, a tomato variety may be more than 100 years old, but if it was developed as a commercial variety, it will never be an heirloom.

yielding plants have more leaves per fruit. Certain large-fruited, potato-leaf varieties, like the legendary pink-fruited 'Brandywine' (see the photo above), tend to have imperfect flowers, so they don't self-pollinate as readily as other tomatoes. Gently flicking your fingers on the flowers should get the pollen where it needs to be. Or try plucking a freshly opened blossom and dabbing it onto other flowers.

Whether heirlooms are more susceptible than hybrids to disease is a topic of debate. Many heirloom devotees say that they aren't. But most modern hybrids do have bred-in disease resistance that heirlooms don't have. To get it, hybridizers use tomato species that have particular genes with high levels of resistance. In my own garden, I haven't seen a marked difference in plant health between hybrids and heirlooms, and most gardeners I know report similar experiences.

SAVE YOUR SEED FOR HEIRLOOM SUCCESS

The key to getting really great heirlooms adapted to your growing conditions is to save your own seed. Many tomatoes improve in flavor with acclimatization. If a variety still doesn't wow you after three years, it might be time to give up on it. At the very least, grow one

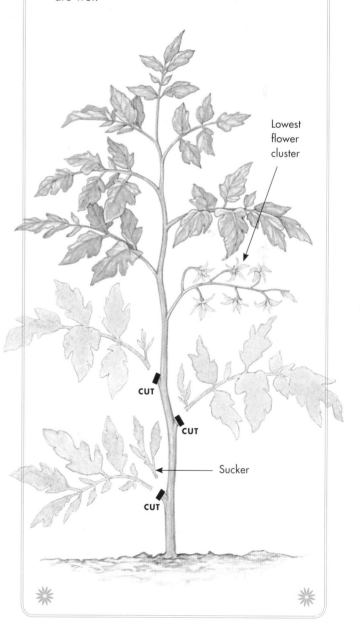

EARLY PRUNING ENCOURAGES STRONG STEMS

Be sure to remove all suckers and leaves below the first flower cluster on your tomato plants. Aside from making the plant stronger, pruning gets it off the ground (helping to ward off diseases) and gives it more room to grow. Never prune tomatoes when the leaves are wet.

Lowest flower cluster

CUT

CUT

Sucker

CUT

generation of seed you have saved yourself. There can be multiple advantages with home-saved seed. One is more tolerance to disease, like early blight. Heavier and earlier fruit set is another plus.

In a small garden, where there may not be room to separate varieties by several feet, you can guarantee self-pollination by loosely tying squares of row-cover material around a cluster of flowers. Small paper bags work well, too. Be sure to put the protection on before the flowers have fully developed and opened, and take it off once they've dropped. Carolyn Male, the doyenne of heirloom-tomato experts, cautions against growing the trendy, tiny-fruited currant tomatoes if you plan to save seed, because they cross-pollinate easily with other tomatoes.

By the time you've grown a few generations of tomatoes from saved seed, part of your heirloom's past will be your own.

TROUBLE-FREE
CHERRY TOMATOES

Cherry tomatoes offer big taste in a small package—and these little favorites are less problematic than larger varieties. For healthy plants and prolific yields, give them what they like best: full sun, fertile soil, and even moisture. With gardener Alice Krinsky Formiga's tips, you'll be gobbling up tomatoes by the handful in no time.

MY 96-YEAR-OLD GRANDMOTHER, JINX, WHEN ASKED THE SECRET of her longevity, advises: "Never say can't, try everything once, and make one new friend each year." She should add growing cherry tomatoes to her litany. Other than walking the dog or taking a language class, I've found that the best way to increase my circle of friends is to grow cherry tomatoes. When they start ripening, I place small baskets of these multicolored sweets around the office. Without fail, people I've never met before approach me to say how much they enjoyed a particular variety, and I invite them to visit my garden for more.

Cherry tomatoes are easygoing fruits that, if grown right, will yield basket after basket of flavorful harvests. They are less prone to many of the problems that plague larger-fruited varieties, and they often produce fruit early.

They may be small, but they're supersweet. Cherry tomatoes are known for their unique, fruity flavor. They're also easy to grow, even in warmer zones.

'Sun Gold'

'Golden Nugget'

'Santa F1'

ABOVE LEFT Don't let the color fool you. 'Green Grape' is an heirloom with excellent flavor that's sweeter than its green or yellow skin implies.

ABOVE RIGHT They may look like grapes, but they're not. Diminutive currant tomatoes grow in clusters of gold or red.

CHOOSE VARIETIES FOR YOUR REGION AND TASTES

If you've never outgrown your desire to play with food, multicolored cherry tomatoes will appeal to you. You can choose colors ranging from yellow to orange to pink or green and varieties with a round, oval, pear, or pointed shape. Because there are so many, I chose my favorites based on their flavor and their suitability for different climates—an important factor in areas with difficult growing conditions.

'Sun Gold' (see the photo above left), an orange hybrid, has attracted a cult following because of its burst of warm, sweet flavor, reminiscent of tropical fruit. Most of the people who tried the fruit in my garden last year could not stop eating them and decided to grow their own this season. 'Sun Gold' has received good reviews from across the country, including states as hot as Alabama. Expect fruit early and often.

'Golden Nugget' is another excellent choice where nights are cool. Developed in Oregon, this variety has tasty yellow fruit that does not require night temperatures above

55°F, as most varieties do. 'Golden Nugget' ripens fast and resists cracking. Determinate in habit and, therefore, compact, it is well suited to growing in containers.

'Green Grape' heirloom tomatoes (see the top left photo on the facing page) are actually green and yellow when ripe (you can tell because they become softer and slip easily off the stem). Put them on your crudité platter to complete the mosaic of colors, or use them to make bright green salsa and ketchup.

Tiny currant tomatoes (see the top right photo on the facing page) come in red, pink, and yellow. Their fruit tends to be seedy but has a distinctive sweet-and-sour flavor. Seed savers should be aware that because of the shape of their flowers, currant tomatoes are more likely to cross-pollinate with other varieties, so seeds saved from nearby tomatoes might not come true. If you plan to save seeds, set the plants at least 50 feet away from other varieties.

Other types of cherry tomatoes that have become more widely available in the past few years are oval shaped. One such variety is 'Santa F1', a hybrid from China. You'll find similar oval tomatoes sold at markets as grape tomatoes.

GIVE CHERRIES FULL SUN AND REGULAR WATERING

Growing cherry tomatoes is easier than growing many large-fruited tomatoes, primarily because cherries produce so many blossoms that there's a good chance some will set fruit, even in less-than-ideal conditions.

Start cherry-tomato seeds indoors on a warm surface six to eight weeks before the last expected frost date in your area. If it never freezes in your zone, start them six to eight weeks before night temperatures are consistently above 50°F. Use a fine seed-starting mix, and sow seeds ¼ inch deep and 2 inches apart. Water so that the soil is moist but not soggy, and keep the soil temperature between 70°F and 90°F. A seed-starting mat gives consistent bottom heat and provides the warmth the seeds need to germinate.

When you see the first signs of life—usually within a week or two—provide strong light. Most gardeners don't have a full day of intense sunlight pouring in through their windows, especially in early spring, so I'd advise against setting your seedlings on the windowsill. Position a grow light 2 to 4 inches away from seedlings for up to 18 hours a day. This should prevent plants from getting leggy.

CHERRY TOMATOES ARE PERFECT CONTAINER PLANTS

All cherry tomatoes can be grown in containers. Use a 5-gallon pot with drainage holes at the bottom. Fill the pots with a planting mixture that drains well. Plant one tomato per pot in a sunny location protected from strong winds.

Water and nutrients leach quickly out of containers. Feed them every two weeks and keep the soil evenly moist, but don't let the pots sit in a saucer full of water. A good fertilizer to use with container tomatoes should have more phosphorus than nitrogen. Too much nitrogen can result in abundant leaves and few fruits. Unless you are growing a dwarf variety, provide a stake or cage to support the sprawling vines.

If you buy nursery-grown plants, find the stockiest ones you can, without flowers or fruit. If only lanky plants are available (left), don't despair. Bury them sideways several inches deeper than they were in the pots (below left). The plants will reach skyward, and more roots will develop along the buried stems.

Once all the plants are up, high temperatures are no longer necessary or desirable, and 60°F to 70°F days and 55°F nights are ideal. When the second set of leaves appears, it's time to transplant. Loosen the roots with a pencil, and transplant seedlings into 4-inch-diameter pots or deep flats. When night temperatures are above 50°F and all danger of frost is past, gradually acclimate your plants to the outdoors.

When they're ready to live outside, prepare a garden bed by adding plenty of manure and a source of phosphorus and calcium (such as bonemeal). Set seedlings 2 to 3 feet apart in rich, well-drained soil, and water them in well.

Like regular tomatoes, cherries need a consistent supply of water. How much you need to water depends not only on the amount of rainfall you receive but also on your type of soil. If you have fast-draining soil, you'll need to keep a close eye on your plants and water often if the weather's been dry. Before watering, check the soil for dryness. If the foliage looks limp, you've waited too long.

Once the plants are established and about a foot tall, lay down mulch. I wait until the plants are this size because they are better able to withstand damage by slugs or other insects that you might find under mulch. Either straw or compost makes a good mulch.

Indeterminate, or vining, cherry-tomato varieties need strong supports. I like to prune the vines to two branches and wind them up strings supported by a wooden frame, for neat appearance, good air circulation, and easy access to the fruit. Caging requires the least work, however, and often produces an even greater yield. Use strong cages made of concrete reinforcing wire, and stake them firmly into the ground; you'll be glad later. Those flimsy inverted conical cages sold at garden centers bend and fall over under the weight of mature plants.

FIGHT DISEASE AND CRACKING WITH CONSISTENT MOISTURE

If tomato-leaf diseases are a problem in your area, choose a variety described as resistant and vigorous. Rotate your crops, because many diseases survive for several years in the soil.

Watering the soil rather than the leaves and mulching the ground with straw will keep the water from splashing onto the lower leaves and stems. This can help prevent diseases from spreading. Some gardeners even remove the lower leaves of tomato plants once they are well established to prevent them from picking up diseases from the ground.

I plant herbs like cilantro and dill near my tomatoes and let them go to flower. They attract beneficial insects that keep pests, such as hornworms, under control.

Cherry tomatoes are less prone to many of the cosmetic problems—blossom-end rot, catfacing, and sunscald—that plague larger-fruited types. Certain varieties are more prone to cracking than others, including most currant tomatoes, which often do better during hot, dry summers.

At harvest time, loose, ripe cherry tomatoes overflow into my hands, but plants often produce so much fruit that it's hard to keep up. Now's the time to start leaving baskets of fruit in strategic locations around the office or to recruit children to help pick. It's amazing how many children who won't touch larger varieties will eagerly reach for cherries.

TOMATO SHAPES AND SIZES

Danielle Sherry explains tomato sizes from smallest to largest.

CURRANT

The tiniest of all tomatoes, currants typically bear fruit in large sprays of grapelike clusters. Individual fruit are usually no bigger than ½ inch in diameter.

CHERRY

Ranging in size from ½ inch to 2 inches in diameter, cherry tomatoes are usually round and come in a variety of colors.

PLUM

This group encompasses the paste tomatoes, which are usually elongated. Within this group are subgroups of shapes, including the pear and fig. Some plums have a pronounced pointed tip.

GLOBE

Globes have the typical tomato shape, with spheres that are generally about the size of a baseball. They can be extremely smooth or can have some slight ribbing on the exterior.

OXHEART

Heart-shaped, oxhearts are usually larger than plums (although similar in shape), weighing in at a pound or more. The flesh is usually meaty, like a beefsteak.

BEEFSTEAK

If one word could describe this group, it would be "behemoth." The fruit of beefsteaks are generally wider than they are long. Irregular shapes and pitting is normal, and all sport meaty flesh.

TOMATOES IN A POT

Colorful, ripe tomatoes can be at your fingertips anytime. The right container, the right soil, and the right variety get you an earlier harvest in any sunny spot, says gardener Sandra B. Rubino.

WHEN MY HUSBAND RETIRED FROM THE NAVY AND WE SET ABOUT gardening on a plot located in Florida's panhandle, tomatoes were high on our list of things to grow. We tried valiantly to rise above our soil, a highly acidic and wormless sand. We built raised beds, added organic fertilizers, and made compost as fast as we could gather leaves and grass clippings. We planted our tomatoes and tended them carefully. They grew, sometimes to astounding size. But they always fell victim to the bacterial wilt endemic to our soil. The tomatoes of our dreams—meaty and juicy with a balance of sweetness and acidity—always eluded us.

We knew that growing tomatoes in the usual way would never produce anything but frustration. Thus, we began to experiment with growing tomatoes in pots. The work came to involve not just soil but also tactics to fend off high humidity, broiling heat, frosts, and insects. Our efforts evolved into a system that works well in our small space.

With the right technique, a container can be transformed into a deliciously convenient tomato garden.

FIND THE RIGHT CONTAINER

We began with terra-cotta pots and whiskey half barrels. Both proved impractical. Clay pots large enough to retain water for more than an hour in late July were too heavy to move and troublesome to sanitize at the end of the season. The half barrels were even more unwieldy. They provided a haven for wood roaches—which like tomatoes almost as much as we do—and they were also susceptible to termites.

When the barrels fell apart in the third year, we sighed with relief and purchased 20-inch-diameter plastic pots and saucers. They are colored and styled to look like old-fashioned terra-cotta. At the end of each year, we scrub them to remove most of the dirt, mold, and algae, then drop them into our heavily chlorinated swimming pool for cleaning. Dollies my husband made allow us to move the potted tomato plants around the patio with ease.

Good drainage and healthy roots go together. At first, we tried layering pebbles in the bottom of each pot. At the end of the season, however, we wanted to dump the exhausted potting mix into our raised-bed vegetable garden. Deliberately adding rocks to our garden beds seemed perverse. The layer of pebbles in the pot also seemed to inhibit root growth. So we moved the river rock into the saucer instead. But we also line the bottom of each pot with a layer or two of plastic window screening so that our soil stays put and drains well. In heavy rains, we siphon the liquid from the saucers with a turkey baster demoted from the kitchen, getting rid of the standing water that mosquitoes love for breeding.

COOK UP THE PERFECT SOIL MIX

Early in the year, we purchase our potting mix and begin to improve it. We want to provide the tomatoes with the calcium and magnesium they will need later, so we thoroughly blend 1 cup of dolomitic limestone into each 40-quart bag of potting mix. In addition, we stir in ½ cup of iron and trace elements, supplied by a soil conditioner. We store the mixture in covered trash cans to mellow.

Screening lets water—not soil—pass through. Cut the mesh to fit the base of the pot (far left), then place it snugly into the bottom of the container (top left). A layer of stone in the saucer ensures that the roots will never sit in standing water and rot (bottom left).

A rich fertilizer mix spurs growth. The recipe for tomatoes in containers includes (clockwise from top left) iron and trace elements, soy meal, greensand, and kelp meal. Nutrients should be well mixed with soil before the tomato containers are filled.

For the next several months, we turn our attention to growing our seeds to transplant size, with a stocky stem and four to six true leaves. Determinate varieties tend to do better in a pot because of their fairly small, compact size. At planting time, we improve the potting mix again, drawing on a balanced organic fertilizer we've already prepared and stored. The recipe calls for 4 cups of soy meal and 2 cups of blood meal for nitrogen; 3 cups of bonemeal for phosphorus; and 2 cups of kelp meal and 4 cups of greensand for potassium. This homemade blend provides slow-release nutrition. We add 2 cups to each 40-quart bag of potting mix. We improve the potting mix in two stages because the dolomitic limestone can prematurely activate the nitrogen.

TOMATO BASICS

- Select a container that isn't too heavy or too hard to sterilize each year.

- Mix up a custom potting soil by adding nutrients and a soil conditioner.

- Fill the pot with a 6- to 8-inch depth of soil, and plant the tomato at the bottom of the pot.

- Keep trimming away the leaves and filling in around the transplant with soil.

- Build a protective netting cage to ward off insects.

CUT-AND-COME-AGAIN TOMATOES

When my tomato plants seem exhausted in mid- to late summer, I prune them down, leaving just a few short stems that are sprouting suckers. This removes the flea beetle– and fungus-infested old growth. Because it is nearly impossible to improve the weary soil in each pot with my preferred organic amendments, I dissolve magnesium-sulfate crystals in water, along with several tablespoons of calcitic lime, and pour a gallon of the solution into each pot. A week later, I use a liquid fertilizer with an N-P-K ratio of 20-20-20 to get the plants moving again.

In less than a month, small tomatoes will form on new growth; soon, there will be another crop, though not as tasty as the first. Cutting weather-weary plants back, however, is practical only if the plant is healthy. The magnesium and calcitic lime treatment may need to be repeated if leaves lose color or growth seems slow.

We fill each pot with potting soil 6 to 8 inches deep, then plant a transplant at the bottom of the pot. As the tomatoes grow, we trim the leaves from the stem and add more of the enriched soil mix until the pot is filled. This practice helps build root mass along the stem as it is buried, which is similar to laying the stem in a trench.

This method also allows us to plant earlier. Because the plants stay below the pot rim for a couple of weeks, we can surround the plants with insulating fabric if there's a cold snap, or cover them with old shower curtains if there's a deluge. Best of all, we can tie layers of nylon netting over each pot to keep early insect marauders at bay.

KEEP INSECTS OUT WITH NETTING

When the pots are filled with soil, we insert a cylinder cage made of concrete reinforcing wire to give the plant support. For the final touch, we use black nylon netting as a defense against insect pests. We buy two 72-inch-wide yards for each pot and enclose the cage with netting, clipping it in place with clothespins around the rims. Heavy rubber bands keep the top closed. Whiteflies and aphids can still get through the netting, but really voracious predators, like tomato worms and stink bugs, are kept out. This slight edge can mean the difference between success and disappointment. Tomatoes generally self-pollinate, so keeping bees out isn't an issue.

We learned this lesson the hard way when we took a week off to visit our son. We arranged for watering, but nothing could protect our plants from the ravages of caterpillars during our absence. When we returned, we found hundreds chewing away, and even quick action with *Bacillus thuringiensis* (Bt) could not undo the damage. The netting also helps keep the sun's rays from scalding the fruit.

Some vigilance is still required, for an occasional enterprising moth will succeed in laying an egg or two. The damage becomes apparent when mysterious holes show up in a leaf here and there. Insecticidal soaps and Bt can be applied through the netting. We need only to unclip the clothespins to side-dress our plants, prune, or pick the fruit.

We never mind the work involved with this process because of the rewards. Every time we sit down to a bowl of bright red fruit, sun warmed and gently seasoned with salt and pepper, oil and vinegar, basil, and a whisper of oregano, it's sunshine in a bowl.

Cage tomatoes for their own good. Concrete reinforcing wire provides sturdy support for tomato vines and a perfect frame to attach antibug netting.

GROWING IN A POT IS DIFFERENT FROM GROWING IN THE GROUND

In some ways, it's more challenging to grow tomatoes in pots, but in other ways, it's far better. Soil in containers warms up quicker than ground soil, so the same variety can ripen up to two weeks earlier in a pot than it would in the ground. If you live in a cool zone with a short summer season, container growing is a great way for you to finally get a decent harvest. Container growing, however, does require more work. You'll have to fertilize more (at least every 10 days because of sharper drainage) and water more. Mulch the top of the pot or cover the outside of the pot (burlap works well) to protect the root system from high heat. I also generally plant short-season tomatoes and small-fruiting varieties in containers because huge beefsteaks need optimal conditions for the entire summer season to produce well in a pot.

GREAT
SAUCE TOMATOES

Homemade tomato sauce is guaranteed to taste better with tomatoes fresh from your garden. The right conditions and a handful of dependable varieties will give you the best flavor. Check out farmer Kris Wetherbee's recommendations.

WHEN I WAS A GIRL, MY MOM AND I TOOK WEEKLY TRIPS TO THE market for fruits and vegetables. Even then, I was fascinated by the different apples, lettuce, peppers, and tomatoes—although there was just one kind of paste tomato, and it was always called 'Roma'.

Gardening and canning have since become a minor obsession and a favorite pastime of mine, and I've realized that it's not just one variety of paste tomato that results in the tastiest salsa, the creamiest ketchup, or the richest spaghetti sauce. That's when I decided to put paste tomatoes to the test. I scrutinized the catalogs and talked with local market growers and gardeners. For the next two years, I grew 20 varieties in my garden so that I could discover for myself if there really was any difference.

Homegrown paste tomatoes
make for delicious sauce.

STICK TO A FEW TRIED-AND-TRUE TYPES

Naturally, flavor is a big factor in what makes a tomato great, but disease resistance, productivity, texture, and ripening time are also important. It doesn't matter how flavorful a tomato is if the growing season is over long before it ripens. The varieties that are tops in my book are 'Black Prince', 'Early Cascade', 'Italian Gold', 'Saucy', and 'Sausage'. Each produces well and has great flavor in good and bad growing seasons alike. These five can be grown in any region where the average tomato can ripen, especially when you are starting with seedlings.

Originally from Siberia, 'Black Prince' has a rich, deep garnet color I love. Like a chameleon, the color changes depending on where you live. Increased sun and heat encourage a deeper color with an almost chocolate glow. The round, egg-size fruits ripen early on indeterminate but restrained vines. I use 'Black Prince' fresh in salads and pasta dishes or combined with 'Viva Italia' for sensational salsa.

'Early Cascade' is an early, disease-resistant, and vigorous plant that performs especially well when staked or caged. It produces an almost continuous bumper crop of rounded, slightly heart-shaped fruit right until the end of the season.

'Italian Gold' puts on a showstopping performance with its beautiful golden yellow fruit and prolific yields. Easy to peel, this tomato is high in pectin, and its refreshing taste makes it perfect for canning and freezing.

No paste tomato is perfect for every need, but 'Early Cascade' and 'Italian Gold' come close. The fruit is a match for just about every use, although 'Early Cascade' may not produce the thickest ketchup and sauces. Because both are easy to peel, they are also the best for canning.

When space is at a premium, plant 'Saucy'. Its determinate, disease-resistant vines are compact but prolific. The easy-to-peel fruit grows in clusters that hold well on the vine until you're ready for them. Use 'Saucy' for salsa making or canning.

'Sausage' really surprised me for several reasons. The indeterminate plant can grow quite tall, and the meaty fruit, shaped like its namesake, can grow up to 6 inches long. A dependable heirloom variety, 'Sausage' comes into full production later in the season, when there is less garden work and more time to devote to preserving the harvest.

OPTIMAL CONDITIONS IMPROVE FLAVOR

Even the most flavorful variety can suffer an unsavory fate when raised in an environment with too much of some things or not enough of others. Too much nitrogen will encourage foliage growth at the expense of fruit production. Excess water can affect flavor, so don't overwater once tomatoes have reached their full size and are beginning to change color. Other factors that can weaken tomato flavor are insufficient heat and light. Always give tomatoes your sunniest spot; they need six hours or more of direct sun a day.

If finding a spot with adequate sun is a problem, try bringing more light and heat to your plants by laying down mulch. To increase the amounts of light and heat that reach the fruit, stake, trellis, or cage your plants. Also, if possible, lighten heavy clay soil by working in compost or other organic materials. In addition to benefitting the harvest, the organic matter will open up the soil, allowing air and water to penetrate better.

A soil test can go a long way in helping you determine how much fertilizer to apply to your plants. Tomatoes require ample amounts of phosphorus, potassium, and calcium, and even though you shouldn't overdo the nitrogen, it is also needed for healthy plants. My plants get a side dressing of well-rotted manure, but compost also works. Rock dust applied at the rate of 10 pounds per 100 square feet or a kelp foliar spray will add plenty of valuable flavor-producing trace minerals.

Once your plants are established, water deeply and keep the soil moisture even; mulching will reduce water loss. When soil moisture fluctuates, blossom-end rot may develop in susceptible plants. This is commonly caused by a calcium deficiency, and moisture fluctuations can interfere with the uptake of calcium. A calcium imbalance can also occur if the soil has too much magnesium, so don't use dolomitic limestone, which is high in magnesium. Before planting, add crushed eggshells or oyster shells to the soil to help prevent the problem.

Experience has shown me that the best salsa or spaghetti sauce has as much to do with the type of tomato used and how it was grown as it does with the recipe. For flavorful food that's hard to resist, grow the best in paste tomatoes.

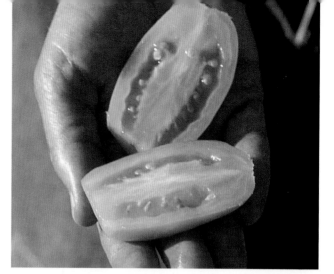

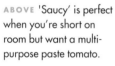**ABOVE** 'Saucy' is perfect when you're short on room but want a multi-purpose paste tomato.

RIGHT 'Sausage' produces prolifically during the latter part of the season, when you're ready to harvest and can.

BELOW LEFT 'Black Prince' is a handsome tomato with rich color and flavor.

TOP 'Italian Gold' has many fine qualities, including firm flesh, good looks, and decent disease resistance.

ABOVE 'Early Cascade' offers vigorous plants and an early season harvest.

LEFT Mulch tomatoes to help prevent moisture fluctuation, which can lead to blossom-end rot.

WHICH STAKES
ARE RIGHT FOR YOU?

*You won't have any trouble choosing the right support once you learn
the pros and cons of six different types from gardener Joe Queirolo.*

SOMETIMES I THINK THERE MUST BE TOMATO SAUCE FLOWING
through my veins. My earliest memories are of watching my
parents water the tomato vines in the backyard and of my Italian
grandfather, who boasted about the big, heavy, delicious tomatoes
he had grown in rocky soil enriched with countless wheelbarrows
full of horse manure. As a kid, I even spent summers at my aunt
and uncle's ranch, where they grew nearly a hundred acres of
processing tomatoes.

These days, tomatoes are still a large part of my life, and summer
would simply not be summer without them. To keep my tomato plants
happy and productive, I give them the necessities of life: food, water,
and light. But for the greatest yields, they also require some means
of support or trellising. Lifting and supporting the plants keeps the
fruit clean and away from pests, provides better air circulation to help
prevent disease, and makes it easier to see and harvest the fruit. I can
also fit more plants into a smaller area by trellising them. During my
many summers of tomato fixation, I've observed and tried many types
of tomato supports and have found several tried-and-true structures
that are readily available, dependable, and sure to keep the garden
looking attractive and orderly.

TOP Florida weave   FAR LEFT Cage   NEAR LEFT Tripod

TOMATO CAGES ARE EASY TO FIND

Tomato cages, structures that entirely encircle a plant, are the easiest supports to use. There are several variations of cages available, but if you're going to be growing just a few plants, the easiest cage to find is the ubiquitous, inexpensive, cone-shaped, heavy-gauge wire tomato basket. Each cage costs just a couple of dollars, and in spring, I see them for sale everywhere, from nurseries to drugstores. You simply push the legs into the soil around a young plant, then let nature take its course. As the plant grows and fills the basket, tuck wayward stems behind the encircling wire. But be careful: These 3-foot-tall cones are not particularly stable. Indeterminate tomato vines can quickly grow beyond the top ring of the basket and topple the whole plant. It is best to use determinate tomato varieties with these cages or be prepared to brace them with stakes when the vines get larger (see the bottom left photo on p. 60).

To support indeterminate varieties, I prefer to make my own cages out of 5-foot-tall concrete reinforcing mesh that I buy at a home-supply store. Make sure the mesh is large enough to get your hand through while clutching a ripe tomato; a 6-inch-square mesh works for me and is readily available in stores. To make the cage, cut a 4½- to 6-foot-long piece, roll it together so that the ends meet, then secure the ends with wire to make a cylinder with a diameter of 1½ to 2 feet. If you garden in a windy area, consider anchoring the cage to the ground with ground staples or stakes.

One drawback to using tomato cages is that they take up a lot of storage space in the off-season. With my homemade version, I can untie, unroll, and stack the wire, but that is somewhat inconvenient. If your storage space is limited, you might want to consider using circular or rectangular collapsible tomato cages, which fold for easy storage.

STAKES ALLOW FOR EASY PRUNING

If you're looking for earlier and bigger tomatoes and you don't mind the extra work of pinching and tying up indeterminate varieties, you can stake them. Just drive a 6-foot-long redwood or cedar 2×2, a length of sturdy bamboo, or a metal T-post about a foot into the ground, and plant your tomato about 6 inches away from the stake. As the vine grows, train it to a single stem by gently breaking off any side shoots that emerge from the main stem. Tie the stem loosely to the stake with strips of soft cloth or nylon. Loop the material entirely around the stake before tying it around the stem. This will cinch the tie and hold it in place as the plant gets heavier. If the ties start slipping down the stake as your tomatoes grow, you can notch the stake or drive a small nail in the stake to hold the ties up.

A tomato spiral is an elegant alternative to a rustic-looking stake. It is a 5-foot-tall metal corkscrewlike device that you wind your plant around as it grows. You may not need to tie the plant up, but you will still want to pinch out any side shoots. Another attractive type of stake is the tomato ladder, a half cage that looks like a small ladder with V-shaped rungs. Plants grown on these ladders don't need to be pinched into a single stem; as the plant grows, just tie the side shoots to the rungs.

You could also build or buy a tripod (see the bottom right photo on p. 60) or tuteur to provide upscale housing for your plants. You can either place a single plant in the middle of the tripod and train it to three or four main stems by keeping the lowest side shoots and pinching out the rest, or place a plant at the base of each leg of the tripod and train each plant to a single stem, which you would tie to that leg.

TRY THE FLORIDA WEAVE IF YOU HAVE LOTS OF PLANTS

Because I grow hundreds of tomato plants, I need to support them quickly, easily, and inexpensively. To do this, I use a staking method called the Florida weave (see the top photo on p. 60) for both my determinate and indeterminate varieties. I plant the tomatoes in rows, and at the ends of each row, I drive steel T-posts into the ground at an oblique angle. Between the plants, I push 8-foot-tall 1×1 redwood or bamboo stakes as far into the ground as I can, then push them in even farther after watering, when the soil is soft.

As soon as the plants begin to lean over, I make the first layer of the weave by tying untreated twine around one T-post, passing it along one side of the first plant, wrapping it around the stake, then past the next plant,

HOMEMADE CAGES

Wire-mesh fencing with large holes can be used to fashion your own cages.

APPROXIMATE COST: 33 CENTS PER FOOT

STAKES

A tomato plant can be trained on a single wooden stake, or several stakes can be made into a tuteur or tripod.

APPROXIMATE COST: $1 TO $3 EACH

SPIRALS

These 5- to 6-foot-tall metal stakes resemble corkscrews.

APPROXIMATE COST: $6 EACH

STANDARD TOMATO CAGES

These tornado-shaped cages are the easiest supports to find.

APPROXIMATE COST: $1 TO $3 EACH

LADDERS

These sturdy plastic-coated metal supports are similar to cages but have one open side.

APPROXIMATE COST: $60 FOR A SET OF FIVE

COLLAPSIBLE CAGES

These work the same way standard cages do but collapse for easier off-season storage.

APPROXIMATE COST: $10 EACH

OPTIONS FOR TRELLISING YOUR TOMATOES

The type of support structure you choose depends on the growth habit of your tomato plants and how much space you have.

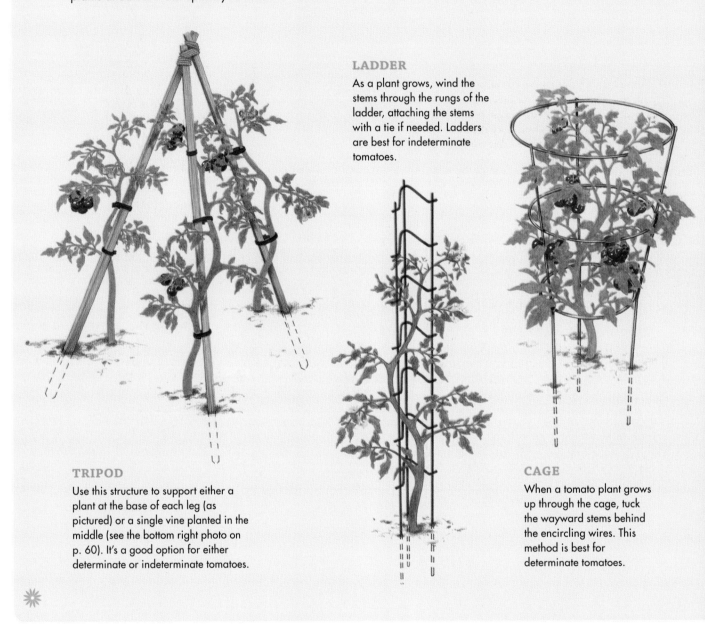

LADDER

As a plant grows, wind the stems through the rungs of the ladder, attaching the stems with a tie if needed. Ladders are best for indeterminate tomatoes.

TRIPOD

Use this structure to support either a plant at the base of each leg (as pictured) or a single vine planted in the middle (see the bottom right photo on p. 60). It's a good option for either determinate or indeterminate tomatoes.

CAGE

When a tomato plant grows up through the cage, tuck the wayward stems behind the encircling wires. This method is best for determinate tomatoes.

around the next stake, and so on. When I reach the T-post at the end of the row, I bring the twine back along the other side of the plants, repeating the process to hem them in so that they are sandwiched between the lengths of twine.

I don't need to prune plants trained this way; I just need to keep weaving and binding the stems with twine. I do this each time the plants grow a foot or so, which works out to about four times a season for indeterminate varieties and maybe twice for determinate ones. If

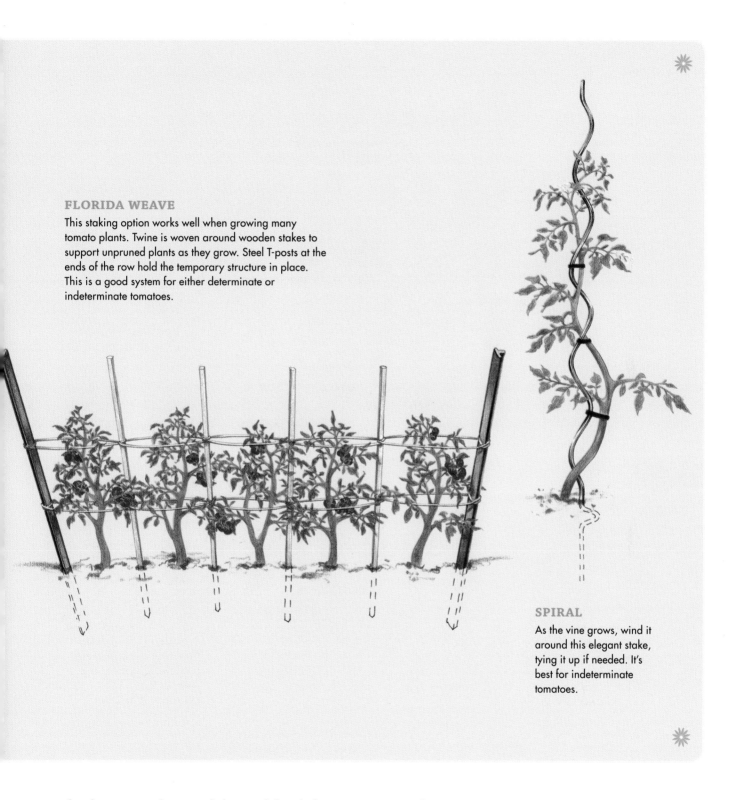

FLORIDA WEAVE

This staking option works well when growing many tomato plants. Twine is woven around wooden stakes to support unpruned plants as they grow. Steel T-posts at the ends of the row hold the temporary structure in place. This is a good system for either determinate or indeterminate tomatoes.

SPIRAL

As the vine grows, wind it around this elegant stake, tying it up if needed. It's best for indeterminate tomatoes.

the plants get too heavy with fruit and the whole row threatens to fall over, I stretch a strong wire between the T-posts and fasten the stakes to it. At the end of the season, I simply cut the twine, remove the stakes, and compost the remaining heap.

When it comes to supporting tomatoes, keeping the fruit off the ground is my main goal, and trellising helps me find my holy grail of summer gardening: a basketful of perfect—and perfectly ripe—tomatoes.

3

PEPPERS & VINES

A BOUNTY OF
BELL PEPPERS

From seedlings to harvest, farmer Alex Hitt teaches you the ABCs of a great pepper crop. Turns out a well-prepared bed and occasional nutrient boosts are the keys to sweet success.

IT'S DINNERTIME. SHOWTIME. TIME TO GO OUT TO THE GARDEN. For eating and entertainment, our diverse cast of bell peppers can't be beat. The rows fill with rainbows as the fruits mature in late summer under dark green canopies of foliage. Some are so sweet that we eat them like apples. What we don't eat fresh, we freeze, so they're available all year. Without the color, texture, and flavor of peppers, why cook? We've developed a system to grow great plants, allowing us to pick peppers over the entire harvest season, which lasts through much of the fall. The production, which is no more than good planning and the usual TLC, is well worth the price.

Every color has a different taste. Healthy conditions ensure a robust crop of bell peppers, regardless of what variety you choose to grow.

GOOD SOIL AND STRONG SEEDLINGS

Peppers are in the ground longer than any other annual. To keep a crop growing strong and weed-free that long requires good planning and attention to the crop's special needs. We pick a planting site where we have not grown tomatoes, eggplant, or potatoes for at least three years. These plants share many of the same soil and leaf diseases, so it's best to avoid giving them a chance to build up.

Peppers grow best in well-drained loam. The heavier the soil, the more organic matter you'll need to add. Any balanced garden soil grows fine peppers. Still, I highly recommend a soil test every few years to assure adequate mineral nutrients, especially phosphorus, which helps roots develop; potassium; and calcium. Additional potassium and calcium might be needed to spur good fruit development. These two nutrients help produce nice, thick pepper walls. Any nutrients should be added in fall.

Eight weeks before transplanting, we start our seeds in a well-drained potting mix and keep them moist and warm (70°F to 80°F) to ensure good germination. We use a heating mat under the seedling flats. But any consistently warm place will work. Plants need to be separated in the seed flat by at least 2 inches for the best growth. After the first true leaves develop, we start fertilizing with a balanced liquid solution, such as a fish emulsion and kelp mixture. Closely watch the cotyledons (the seed leaves that appear before the first true leaves). They should be vibrant and green; yellow cotyledons indicate insufficient nitrogen. It's best to gradually expose transplants to the outdoors for a week or two prior to setting them out.

MAKE THE BED THE RIGHT WAY

Three to four weeks before transplanting, we incorporate some nitrogen into the bed. Peppers need about 1 pound of nitrogen per 500 square feet. We also install a drip-irrigation line down the middle of the bed and cover the bed with black landscape fabric, pinning the edges down securely to prevent the fabric from blowing up in high winds. We make 4-inch-diameter holes in the fabric (see the photo above); the edges can be melted with a candle so that they won't unravel. We prefer landscape fabric over plastic. Because landscape fabric is permeable, water won't puddle on top and become a catalyst for disease.

Good rows grow good plants. We plant peppers in two rows per bed, with the rows 12 inches apart and the plants 18 inches apart in the row. This promotes good airflow

Black fabric suppresses weeds and moderates soil temperatures, helping the peppers thrive.

among the plants for disease control and high production. Between the beds, we leave a wide path mulched with straw. This provides room for the plants to grow and eases access for picking. The mulch helps ripen the fruit evenly by reflecting light on the underside of the peppers.

Mulch also keeps the soil cooler and the humidity up a little. While peppers need heat to get going fast and early, they will not set fruit if it's too hot. Nighttime temperatures over 80°F and daytime temperatures over 95°F will cause flowers to drop or fail to produce viable pollen. Light-colored mulch in the paths may help overcome this by reflecting some heat.

TRANSPLANT WHEN IT IS WARM

On transplanting day, we hope for clouds, cool temperatures, and no wind. We give the plants a good watering with a fertilizer solution just before we set them out. The weather can't be too cool, however. Peppers hate cold temperatures, both in the air and in the soil. When you transplant, you want the plants to keep growing vigorously. Pepper plants sulk in nighttime temperatures below 55°F and soil temperatures below 65°F.

Using a trowel, we set the young plants through the holes in the landscape fabric. Peppers, unlike their tomato cousins, won't grow more roots from their stems if buried deeply. But they support themselves better if they are planted a bit deeper than in the seedling flat. In hot climates with sandy soils, you can plant them up to the first true leaves, thus putting their roots down into cooler, moister soil. The heavier the soil, the shallower

MY PERFECT PEPPERS

When it comes to peppers, you can never plant enough. They're an essential culinary ingredient in several of my favorite recipes. Although they may look similar, their flavor varies greatly. Here are a few of my favorite peppers whose taste is tops. —PATTI MORENO

CALIFORNIA WONDER

DESCRIPTION: A medium-size green bell pepper

WHY I LOVE THEM: This crunchy and sweet midseason veggie is the perfect go-to pepper when you need one in your recipe. It's tasty even before it ripens.

'California Wonder'

CORNO DI TORO GIALLO & CORNO DI TORO ROSSO

DESCRIPTION: Large, 8-inch-long yellow and red heirloom Italian peppers, which sport a bullhorn (corno di toro) shape that tapers at the end

WHY I LOVE THEM: They are sweet, spicy, and unique looking. The plants produce tons of fruit, so they're perfect to share.

MINI RED BELL

DESCRIPTION: An early variety that produces peppers that are 1½ to 2 inches across

WHY I LOVE THEM: It is perfect for stuffing. This pepper plant is

great for areas with a short growing season, and its short stature (2 feet tall) makes it perfect for a patio container.

'Mini Red Bell'

QUADRATO D'ASTI GIALLO & QUADRATO D'ASTI ROSSO

DESCRIPTION: Four-lobed, medium-size yellow (giallo) and red (rosso) Italian peppers with thick walls

WHY I LOVE THEM: These are the perfect peppers to use in salads or your favorite sausage-and-peppers recipe.

they should be planted to reduce the risk of stem blight that develops in waterlogged ground. If you give your peppers 1½ to 2 inches of water a week, they should start blooming like crazy several weeks after transplanting.

PICKING PEPPERS TAKES PRECISION

Good crop rotation, the use of disease-resistant varieties, and good air circulation take care of 95 percent of our pest problems. That leaves the major antagonist: caterpillars—both the European corn borer and the corn earworm—which fly in as moths and lay eggs on the peppers. They become a problem in mid-July, after they've had their fill of everyone's corn and about the time our peppers appear.

We spray reluctantly and only if damage goes beyond our tolerance. We use *Bacillus thuringiensis* (Bt), a naturally occurring bacterium that attacks the worms' digestive system. Most years, one treatment does the trick. Other than water, the peppers may need a little nitrogen boost late in the season. When the leaves begin to lose that dark green color, we consider feeding them.

Fifty to 60 days after transplanting, we begin picking peppers. For the colored sweet bells, we pick the first green peppers that appear low on the plant because experience has taught us that fruit rot invades if we let them go to color. For the first two to three weeks of fruiting, we pick the first pepper produced at the first fork in the plant, then move up the plant and thin the fruit so that they are not touching and have good airflow around them. By August 1, we stop picking the immature green peppers and wait for them to turn their vibrant colors. For almost the next two months, there's a weekly harvest. The curtain falls with the first hard freeze, and we start looking forward to the next season.

CHILES LIKE IT HOT

Some are mild, others can burn you alive, but no matter your taste, you can find a chile or two to spice up your cooking. Gardeners Lee James and Wayne James share their secret to thriving plants.

UNTIL RECENTLY, IF YOU WANTED TO ADD A LITTLE FIRE TO YOUR food, you didn't have many choices. You could grind black pepper over your plate or shake on some dried red chile flakes.

Lately, however, the whole topic of spicy ethnic foods has gotten hotter than a habanero. Authentic Mexican food, Thai cuisine, and Hunan dishes are all the rage—and they all use some type of chile for their heat. Consequently, you'll find that most supermarkets have a variety of hot chile sauces on their shelves and lots of fresh chiles in their produce section.

The sudden popularity of chile peppers is good news for the vegetable gardener: Almost every seed catalog you open now lists lots of hot chile varieties.

You've probably heard that variety is the spice of life. We'll take that a step further and say that growing a variety of chiles will add a whole lot of spice to your life, your kitchen, and your garden. It takes a little work, but you'll be rewarded with a colorful and flavorful abundance of different chiles.

These peppers are hotter than the sun. This variety of New Mexican chile, called mirasol, points up to the sky rather than hanging down like most chiles, but it still packs a punch like all the members of this vegetable group.

SEEDS DON'T MAKE CHILES HOT

A pepper's hotness comes from the capsaicin (*cap-SAY-a-sin*): the light-colored, pulpy membranes (ribs) inside a chile pod's walls. Capsaicin is a tasteless, odorless compound that is insoluble in water. That's why drinking water or chewing on an ice cube won't kill the burning sensation after you eat a particularly fiery chile. To minimize the release of capsaicin, cut the chile in half, rake out the ribs and seeds, and rinse it well.

Seeds

Ribs

Wall

PICK YOUR PEPPER BASED ON YOUR HEAT TOLERANCE

Not all chile types are excruciatingly hot. Some are quite mild and will make your tongue tingle only a little bit. And don't confuse the hotness of a chile with its taste. Taste and heat are two separate sensations, and all chiles have both.

New Mexican chiles (see the top left photo on the facing page) are only mildly hot. If you peruse seed catalogs, you'll see that New Mexican, Anaheim, or long green and red chiles are all the same type. Call them what you will, all varieties of this type of chile have productive, 12- to 20-inch-tall plants. Some pods hang down, while others, known as mirasol, point straight up. Expect up to 75 pods per plant. New Mexican chiles are used fresh as green chiles, but when they ripen red, they get sweeter and hotter.

Poblanos (see the bottom left photo on the facing page) are large, mild-tasting chiles that are excellent in chile rellenos—whole chiles stuffed and fried in a fluffy egg batter. The plants are not particularly productive; even the new, improved varieties often grow fewer than

10 pods per plant. Poblanos have thin walls, making them perfect for drying. After they ripen, having turned from dark green to bright red, you can string the chiles together and hang them in the sun or other dry place, then use them throughout the year. When they are dried, poblanos are called anchos.

Hungarian wax chiles (see the center left photo on the facing page) are bright yellow, and they have a mild flavor that is more like a sweet pepper than a hot chile. There are medium-hot and hot varieties. The plants are very productive, and they set pods early, making them good for northern gardens. Most will ripen to luscious reds and oranges that are deliciously sweet.

Cayennes, both red and gold, are best for adding just-plain heat to anything. The plants are small, but they produce plenty of chiles that ripen early. One or two small plants will provide enough for the year. Their thin skins make them excellent drying chiles.

Jalapeños (see the bottom right photo on the facing page) are probably the best middle-of-the-road chiles because they're not too hot and not too mild. These are the chiles most people imagine when they think of hot peppers. Jalapeños are the standard salsa chile and the canned pepper you see in the Mexican-food section of your supermarket. All jalapeño varieties are productive, growing around 75 pods per plant. Jalapeños can be used green or when they ripen to a bright red color.

Serranos (see the photo on the facing page) are little finger-size bullets of heat. They can be used green, but we think they are best in salsas, sauces, stews, and soups after they ripen to a bright red. The plants are tall and wide, growing up to 3 feet in both directions. Serranos produce pods much later than jalapeños, but when they do, the plants are absolutely loaded.

Most people say habaneros are the hottest type of chile in the world. Many habanero chiles have small squarish pods with lots of folds and crevices. One catalog describes its 'Golden Habanero' as "positively NUCLEAR." Of all the habaneros, the Scotch bonnet (see the top right photo on the facing page) is our favorite small, fiery chile for spicy Asian stir-fries, curry dishes, salsas, and marinades; it still

RIGHT Chiles can have multiple names. Anaheim, New Mexican, and long green and red chiles all refer to the same type of thick-walled, meaty chile.

ABOVE Hungarian wax chiles set pods early. This trait makes them ideal for cooler climates.

RIGHT Plant a pepper worth stuffing. Beefy poblano chiles are called anchos when they're dried and are commonly used whole in dishes.

ABOVE Watch out for the hottest chile of them all. Habaneros are small and puckered, almost as if they were cringing from their own heat. Scotch bonnet habanero (pictured) is milder than most.

ABOVE A color change increases the heat. Mature jalapeño pods are green, but they turn red as they ripen—and get hotter.

Serrano

Habanero

CHILE BASICS

- Start chile seeds in flats eight weeks before you want to transplant them outside.

- Set flats on a germinating heat mat set to 80°F.

- When seeds sprout, place a fluorescent light directly over the seedlings, almost touching them.

- After four weeks, transplant them to small pots and keep them warm.

- After four more weeks, harden them off and plant outside when the garden soil is warm.

- Stake plants to prevent tipping.

- Harvest chiles as they mature to encourage the plant to continue to flower.

Transplanting makes for stronger roots. After the first true leaves open, transplant young chiles from plug trays to larger containers, like the six-packs shown here.

has some of that wonderful, fruity habanero flavor, but it's not as hot as some habaneros. The plants are short and wide, and they set a tremendous number of pods, even in a summer that may not have had enough sun or warm weather to produce other habaneros.

HEAT IS ESSENTIAL FOR SUCCESSFUL SEED STARTING

To start seeds, we spread about 2 inches of a very porous seed-starting mix in a plug tray. Of course, chile seeds need water, but little chile roots can't stand soggy soil and they need oxygen. Make sure your potting mix provides good drainage and aeration. Sprinkle the seeds thinly on top of the mix, then cover them with ½ inch of potting mix.

Put the tray on a germination heat mat, and set the thermostat so that the soil stays at about 80°F. After the seeds sprout, which can take anywhere from five days to two weeks, they'll need a lot of light. If you don't have a greenhouse, place the trays on a windowsill and supplement the natural light with a fluorescent bulb. Keep the lamp almost touching the tops of the plants, raising it as the plants grow.

The two cotyledons, or seed leaves, will open first. At about four weeks, when the next set of leaves opens—the first true leaves—we transplant the seedlings into plastic

STAKE PLANTS TO PREVENT SUNBURN

Chile plants thrive in full sun; in fact, they need full sun so that the pods can ripen. The problem is that the pods can suffer from sunburn, which will make them taste sour. Because chile plants—especially the bigger types, like poblanos—tend to tip over and expose their pods to the hot sun, we stake each plant right after it goes in the ground, then push dirt around it for additional support.

pots or six-packs (see the top photo on the facing page). We find the six-packs to be handier because they make the most out of the space available on the heating mat.

Transplanting helps the chiles develop a strong root system. Strong roots can keep a plant from falling over when it's laden with pods. Adjust the temperature of the heat mat so that the soil stays about 75°F, and keep the lamp right on top of the plants.

Water the seedlings enough to keep the soil evenly moist. Every other watering can be a weak solution—twice the recommended amount of water—of either fish emulsion or a soluble starter fertilizer with low nitrogen (15-25-25). Nitrogen is great for leaf development, but too much nitrogen can hamper the development of the chile plant's pods.

ACCLIMATE YOUR CHILES TO THE GARDEN

If you put chiles in the garden too early, they will not do well. Along with warm nighttime temperatures, you also need garden soil that feels warm up to your wrist when you dig your hand into the ground. If you absolutely can't wait for the weather, you can warm up your soil by covering it with a layer of black plastic.

Hardening off involves gradually decreasing the soil temperature and allowing the soil to dry a little more between each watering. The plants can spend their seventh week outside in their pots if you're sure that nighttime temperatures are at least 45°F.

If night temperatures are consistently above 55°F, you can transplant the chiles outside at about eight weeks. But if the soil is not warm or the nights are still too cold, you should either protect the plants in the garden with some kind of row cover or keep the plants inside a little while longer, fertilizing the pots lightly.

A sunny garden enriched with compost is ideal for chiles. As before, when you were feeding the newly transplanted seedlings, don't use any nitrogen-rich organic additives that might inhibit pod production.

To plant your chiles, use your hand to scoop out a hole that is just a little deeper than the pots. Then set the transplants in these holes, burying the root balls up to the cotyledons. Fill in the hole, and firm down the soil. Continue to water the transplants with the same fertilizer you were using for the seedlings, and you'll be harvesting before you know it.

THE MORE YOU PICK, THE MORE YOU GET

You can start picking your chiles when they are mature, before they ripen to their final color. Except for some yellow chiles, like Hungarian wax, mature chiles are green. Look for a full-size pod, and squeeze it gently. It should be heavy and feel thick and hard. Harvesting chiles as they mature encourages the plant to continue flowering. Your overall production will be greater if you keep picking the mature green chiles.

But don't feel that you need to pick all the pods when they're full grown. As chiles ripen, their flavor, heat, and beauty increase until the chiles reach their final color of dark green, yellow, orange, or red, depending on the type. When a chile reaches its ripe color, it should be harvested; otherwise, it will dry up and get soft. Chile pods are best harvested using clippers or shears. Pulling the pods can tear the plant.

GROWING YOUR OWN
GREEN BEANS

It's all about variety—of the bean, that is. Beyond that, regular watering and frequent picking yield a bountiful harvest. Farmer Melinda Bateman tells you what you need to know.

ONE DAY, AT THE FARMERS' MARKET, A CUSTOMER LOOKED AT MY beans and inquired as to whether I had grown the ones she had eaten the previous night at a local restaurant. I had. She proceeded to rave about how incredible they had been. To her, they were the most memorable part of the meal. Fancy that—green beans being the best part of a delicious meal at a fine restaurant. She bought a pound of beans and went home happy.

What is the allure of green beans? To me, it's their tender, fresh sweetness, that essential flavor condensed into one small package—green-bean perfection. The chefs we sell to love them because these beans really add elegance to a dinner plate. And they are my favorite crop to grow.

We live and farm four miles north of Taos, New Mexico, at an elevation of 7,600 feet. Our average yearly rainfall is 12 inches. We have a four-month growing season and heavy winds in May and June. How can I grow good beans in such an extreme climate? The secret of my success lies in our choice of varieties.

Fresh green beans are
the star of any dish.

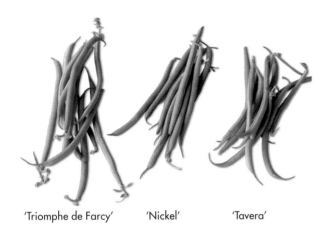

'Triomphe de Farcy'   'Nickel'   'Tavera'

Fertile soil goes a long way. Other than adequate space, beans need rich soil to bush out and produce to their fullest potential.

FERTILE SOIL AND REGULAR MOISTURE ARE CRITICAL

We have trialed numerous varieties and settled on growing those that are considered filet beans. This type of green bean is thinner than other beans. The varieties 'Tavera' and 'Nickel' both bear big crops. These varieties are small seeded—and the smaller the seed, the more tender the bean.

There is another type or class of green bean that has large seeds. I have trialed a number of these: 'Vernandon'; 'Fin des Bagnols'; 'Triomphe de Farcy'; and 'Emerite', a pole-bean type that requires trellising or some kind of support. In our garden, they produce relatively few beans, which are usually large and tough, even when picked daily. I can't recommend them, although I have wondered occasionally if these varieties would do better in a different climate.

For the home gardener, some well-cared-for soil with a light treatment of compost should provide green beans with nearly all the nutrients they need. We water all our crops with drip irrigation, which we lay right beside each row of beans. During the growing season, we run daily cycles of water. The beans get 30 to 45 minutes per day, either in the evening or early morning. This keeps the soil moist but not soggy. You will need to adjust watering to suit your climate conditions.

I wait for the weather to settle before planting green beans. When the soil is warm enough to plant corn (60°F), it's also safe for beans. In cooler soils, beans germinate erratically and the plantings lack vigor. They end up bearing about the same time as later plantings. But you don't need a soil thermometer to know when to plant;

when it feels safe to set out tomatoes, eggplants, and peppers, you can plant beans, too. I can usually sow a first crop by early June. It will begin to yield about 50 days later. I do a series of succession plantings, allowing 10 days to two weeks between plantings. Yields vary with weather conditions, but typically the first week of harvest is scanty, the second week is heavy, and the yield tapers off again the third week. After that, we tear out the beans.

INOCULATE AND SPACE THE SEED FOR A BETTER CROP

Prior to planting, we inoculate bean seeds with nitrogen-fixing bacteria powder. This step allows the beans to produce nitrogen, which leads to a hardier plant, so I think it's worth the time to inoculate. All you need is a clean tin can holding all the beans you plan to plant in the next half hour, a sprinkle of inoculant, and a splash of water to make the inoculant stick to the beans. Give the can a shake, and you're ready to plant (see the top left photo on the facing page). If you don't sow all the seeds you inoculate, let them dry out and store them for another planting.

I plant beans in shallow furrows cut open with the edge of a hoe. I space the seed 2 inches apart, then rake soil over the seeds, burying them under ½ inch of soil. The rows of beans are spaced 18 inches apart. The last step is to turn on the drip system and soak the soil thoroughly.

When the beans are showing their first true leaves (see the top right photo on the facing page), I thin out half the plants and weed the rows. Several weeks later, as the plants bush out, I thin the rows to create an 8-inch spacing between plants and I weed a final time. Once the plants fill out, they shade out most weeds.

FAR LEFT Inoculate bean seed with nitrogen powder. This enables the plant to convert nitrogen in the air to a form usable by plants.

LEFT Thinning is about timing. Once seedlings have their first set of true leaves, they're ready to be thinned so that each plant is 4 inches apart.

Green beans don't tolerate frost and tend to brown, like basil, at about 38°F. Keep this in mind when choosing dates for succession plantings. Make your last planting 80 days before your last frost-free date. If you live where summers get very hot, consider planting green beans in spring or fall, because they lose tenderness in hot weather.

How many beans should you plant at a time? One plant will yield about ½ pound of beans. If I were planting just for our family of four, I would plan on five to 10 plants per planting. To the first planting, I would add three extra plants for seed saving. When they're in season, we eat green beans daily, so adjust your planting accordingly.

PESTS AND DISEASES ARE FEW AND FAR BETWEEN

We have had no real pest problems with beans. One year, I found a few Mexican bean beetle larvae. Oddly enough, they were only on the 'Emerite' beans I was trialing that season. I handpicked the larvae and crushed them.

Limit the handling or harvesting of plants in rainy weather because this can knock off blossoms and decrease your yield. In humid climates, where rust might be a problem, handling wet plants can also transmit rust disease. We began feeding the plants just at blossom set with a foliar spray of kelp, hoping this would encourage the plants to set fruit longer, but we don't yet have any proof of positive results.

We harvest every other day, picking when they are 4 to 5 inches long. Green beans do not keep well, so you should eat them within four days of picking. If you need to store your harvest for a few days, soak the beans in cold water to remove any field heat, then drain them and refrigerate in a plastic bag. But if you love these elegant, tender beans as much as we do, you won't be storing them long.

GROWING BEANS TO SAVE FOR SEED

- Sow a few extra plants with your first planting of green beans, and leave these to make seed. It takes another four to six weeks from the time beans are ready for eating until they're ready to harvest for seed.

- Harvest the pods when they are brown and dry (see the bottom right photo). The seed inside should be hard. Shell out the seeds (see the bottom left photo) by hand, and store them in a paper bag labeled with the varietal name, the original seed source, and the year.

- Bean seeds can keep their vigor for many years. I do a germination check with any seed I am uncertain about, to test the seeds' viability. To do this, I put 10 to 20 seeds on a damp paper towel, roll it up, seal it in a plastic bag, and put it on top of the refrigerator for warmth. A week later, I check for sprouting seeds.

SUPERSWEET
SNAP PEAS

After a long winter of frozen vegetables and bland flavor, peas are a welcome reprieve. Author David Hirsch swears that one bite of snap peas will convince you never to grow any other type again.

IT'S ALWAYS A GREAT DAY WHEN I PICK THE FIRST SNAP PEAS. A lot of the harvest never makes it to the kitchen. Snap peas—which snap like green beans and look and grow just like regular shelling peas—have one delicious difference: The pods are as tender and sweet as the peas inside.

Although something like snap peas grew in the United States more than a hundred years ago, most gardeners didn't know about them until Calvin Lamborn developed 'Sugar Snap' in the late 1970s. Lamborn, a pea breeder for Rogers Seed Company, crossed a sugar pea that had a thin, twisted, edible pod with a shelling pea that had an undesirably thick pod. The result was a pea with a round pod and a crisp, tender, juicy texture. In 1979, 'Sugar Snap' was voted the All-America Selections winner for the best new vegetable, and it has been one of the most popular vegetables to grow ever since. Other varieties of snap peas have been introduced over the years, but 'Sugar Snap' is still my favorite. It has the

The plumper the pea, the sweeter the taste. Snap peas are generally ready for harvest as soon as the pods begin to swell in late spring. You'll also harvest more peas per square foot with snap varieties than you would with traditional types.

LEFT Snap peas fruit until the weather gets hot. For a long harvest, plant seeds six weeks before the last spring frost.

BELOW 'Sugar Snap' has always been tops in taste. Though other sweet varieties of snap peas, such as 'Sugar Ann' and 'Sugar Bon', have been developed since 'Sugar Snap' first came out in the late 1970s, pea growers still insist that 'Sugar Snap' has the best flavor.

sweetest flavor of all the snap peas, and it also supplies a long, abundant harvest, beginning about 10 weeks after sprouting.

PLANT WHEN THE AIR IS COOL AND THE SOIL ISN'T SOGGY

Seed packets tell us to plant peas in the spring as soon as the soil can be worked—when all the frost is gone from the garden beds and the soil isn't too soggy. I would add these warnings: It's essential to plant peas early because the vines stop flowering when daytime temperatures stay above 80°F. On the other hand, if the soil is too cold and wet when you plant, the seeds can rot before they sprout. Pea seeds germinate best when the soil is between 50°F and 75°F.

I aim to plant in mid-April, about six weeks before the last-frost date in my area. I sow the seeds over a two- to three-week period for a nice, long harvest. If April is cold, though, the first plants sulk, and all my plantings begin bearing about the same time. Snap peas aren't that particular about soil. I add compost or rotted manure every year, shoveling about 1 inch on top of the soil and working it in.

Special soil bacteria called rhizobia live in a symbiotic relationship with pea roots and help the plant extract nitrogen from the air. Although snap peas will grow without these bacteria, you can give them a boost and increase yields by inoculating them with rhizobia at planting time. You can usually buy the bacteria through the same catalog from which you order the peas. Dampen the seeds, roll them in the powder, and plant as usual. Some people say you need to inoculate only the first time you plant peas in a particular spot. Others say yields improve enough to justify using pea inoculant every year. I use it every year.

I grow my 'Sugar Snap' peas on a simple trellis system (see the sidebar on p. 87), which runs down the center of a raised bed. The heavy, pea-laden vines grow up to 7 feet tall, and they need a substantial support to keep them from blowing over. While it takes a little extra work to set up a trellis, I notice that, as I get older, I appreciate

PEA BASICS

- Dig 1 inch of compost or manure into the beds.

- Plant early in spring, as soon as the soil is workable.

- Inoculate seeds with rhizobia bacteria.

- Sow the seeds 1 to 2 inches apart and ½ inch deep.

- Harvest when the pods are 3 inches long and plump.

BELOW Prop up dwarf varieties with cut brush or stiff grass. You can use just about anything, including the bamboolike stalks of ornamental miscanthus grass shown here, to keep the short plants from blowing over in the wind.

the comfort of not having to harvest every vegetable squatting, crouching, or bending over.

You don't need a trellis to grow some varieties of snap peas. Good-tasting dwarf varieties, like 'Sugar Ann' or 'Sugar Bon', require little or no help to hold themselves off the ground. Their vines grow 18 to 24 inches tall and bear 2½-inch-long pods about 60 days after planting. The pods are ready to harvest seven to 10 days earlier than 'Sugar Snap' peas.

SOW IN BANDS, NOT IN ROWS

I've found that peas help keep each other propped up if they are planted close together. For dwarf varieties (those that grow less than 3 feet tall), I scatter the seeds an inch or two apart in a 6-inch-wide band, and cover them with ½ inch of soil. As they grow, the plants' tendrils wrap around each other, and the whole clump stays off the ground.

I plant tall peas, like 'Sugar Snap', in a 3-inch-wide band below the trellis (see the left photo below). Once the peas' tendrils catch the bottom of the netting, they will clamber to the top on their own. I keep the soil around the pea vines evenly moist, but I don't mulch because that encourages slugs, which are fond of defoliating the vines. My snap peas haven't been bothered much by any other pests or diseases. The only problem I've had is aphids late in the picking season. They're quickly dispatched with a spray of the hose or insecticidal soap.

By mid- to late spring, the pods are about 3 inches long and ready to pick. Snap peas are at their best when the pods are well rounded and filled with plump peas but before they start to yellow or fade. Once the pods reach this stage, it's best to pick them every other day, because the more you pick, the more you'll get throughout the season.

In summer, when the weather gets hot, the peas stop flowering and producing pods. I cut the vines at the base of the trellis and let them dry for a couple of days so that they'll come off the netting more easily. There's still plenty of growing time to plant salad or cooking greens, root crops, or quick-maturing bush beans in the same spot to follow the dearly departed peas.

Well-spaced trellised snap peas can share their space. Plant the peas down the center of a bed, 1 to 2 inches apart (above). Providing a trellis for the shoots to climb leaves plenty of room on both sides of the plot for other crops (left).

BUILD A SIMPLE TRELLIS

You can set up an inexpensive, 8-foot-long trellis in less than an hour. You'll need two 7-foot-tall metal fence posts and an 8-foot length of nylon trellis netting.

POUND THE POSTS 2 feet into the ground. Then string the netting between them, stretching it tight and tying at even intervals up and down the sides. Pea-laden vines are heavy, so make sure the netting is attached securely.

CUT THE VINES at the base of the trellis at the end of the season, and let them dry out. Pull the dried vines off the netting, and bring the netting inside for winter.

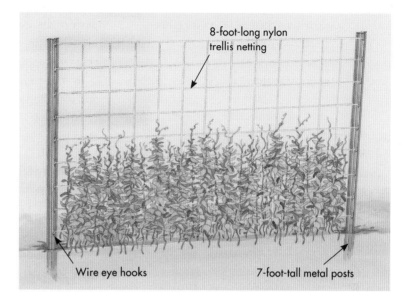

8-foot-long nylon trellis netting

Wire eye hooks

7-foot-tall metal posts

REUSE THE SAME NETTING for up to 10 years. You can also use biodegradable netting instead of nylon, so that you can cut the mesh and pea vines down together and compost the whole thing.

They're ready to pick when the pods swell. If you pick them too soon, you'll find that younger snap peas aren't as sweet.

PICKLING
CUCUMBERS

Compact plants grow faster and produce more fruit than traditional cukes but aren't limited to pickling. Market gardener Cass Peterson knows what it takes to grow these crunchy, sweet veggies.

MY AUNT ELEANOR WAS KNOWN FOR HER PICKLES. SHE MAINtained a large patch of pickling cucumbers, which it was my duty to pick. The patch was a sea of cucumber vines into which I went barefoot, feeling with my toes for the fruit hidden amid a tangle of stems and leaves, every misstep filling the air with the scent of crushed cucumber. A 10-minute search was usually enough to fill a 2-gallon bucket, and I took my reward in a couple of fresh cucumbers—one to eat and one to cut open and rub on legs itching from the plants' spiny foliage. Cucumbers are soothing, inside and out.

Aunt Eleanor had the space to indulge her pickles, but you can enjoy the crunchy goodness of just-picked cucumbers without surrendering the entire garden to their vines. Hybridizers have been making cucumber plants more compact as well as more productive and more resistant to disease. Picklers are prolific and quick to produce, with some varieties bearing fruit in as little as 45 days.

Don't let their small size fool you. Petite pickle cukes offer a sweet, crunchy taste that you won't find with their larger cousins.

Skin color can range widely among varieties. The emerald color of 'Calypso' (above) sets it apart from other picklers, which typically have light-colored stripes or speckles, like 'H-19 Little Leaf' (left).

GREENER ISN'T ALWAYS BETTER

Cucumber varieties come in a range of colors, flavors, textures, and sizes. I like to grow several different varieties to spice things up. One of my new favorites is 'North Carolina Heirloom Pickling' cucumber, a prolific

heirloom with a blocky shape, creamy white skin, and pale chartreuse flesh. It was the first cucumber I was able to harvest, and it had a fantastic, fresh lemony flavor. This variety makes superb dill pickles because it stays crisp when pickled. I also like using it to make a simple cucumber martini.

—KATHY MARTIN, MASS. GARDENER

CERTAIN PICKLERS PROVIDE THE BEST CRUNCH

You don't have to pickle picklers. Harvested young, when the seed cavities are small, any variety of pickler is fine for fresh eating—in a salad or out of your hand. Pickler varieties aren't uniformly dark green like the slicing-type cucumbers sold in the supermarket. They are a paler green, sometimes having light-colored stripes running lengthwise down the fruit. Picklers have thinner skin and crisper, crunchier flesh than most slicers.

Catalog descriptions of vining habits aren't always useful. The word "vigorous" is often used to indicate heavy flowering and fruiting, rather than rampant vines. You won't really know their habit until you try them, but in general, the newer hybrids (picklers as well as standard cucumbers) have shorter vines. In my garden, 'Calypso', 'Royal', and 'H-19 Little Leaf' will travel 4 to 6 feet, but you can turn the vines back on themselves if they stray too far. 'Pickalot' and 'National Pickling' will journey a good 8 to 10 feet from where they're planted, but they, too, can be trained to climb over themselves.

There are dwarf varieties—including 'Bush Pickle Hybrid', with vines only 18 inches long—suitable for

WHAT ARE CUCURBITACINS?

Cucumbers produce natural compounds called cucurbitacins, which are responsible for the bitterness that sometimes develops in the skin. Cucurbitacins are irresistible to cucumber beetles, which home in on the scent to find the plants they love to eat. At high levels, cucurbitacins can cause people stomach distress and give the cucumber a strongly pungent flavor.

BUILDING A BETTER CUKE

Plant breeders have been working to reduce the level of cucurbitacins in cucumbers, with the result being so-called "burpless" cukes. Burpless cucumber varieties produce fewer of the cucurbitacins that people don't like the taste of, and they may be less susceptible to damage from the cucumber beetle.

USING THEM FOR GOOD

Cucurbitacin lures are part of the growing field of Integrated Pest Management. Although some kinks remain, such as how best to deliver the compound, what has worked in research may, one day, be the salvation of home-garden cukes, too.

growing in small spaces or even in containers. Cucumber vines are attractive enough that a pot of them wouldn't look out of place on the patio. 'H-19 Little Leaf' is a particularly good candidate, with its ivylike foliage and clouds of yellow flowers.

Cucumbers have grasping tendrils and will willingly haul themselves up a fence or trellis. If you have limited space but want to grow one of the standard-size pickling hybrids, like 'Calypso', consider growing them vertically.

AVOID PESTS, BUT ENCOURAGE FERTILITY

The cucumber beetle, $1/5$ inch long, either spotted or striped, is the worst enemy of cucumbers, especially in the Midwest and East. It is attracted to the scent of cucurbitacins, which are produced by cucumbers, squash, melons, and other cucurbits. Adult beetles feed on flowers and foliage; their larvae feed on roots. Worse, the beetles may infect the plant with a disease called bacterial wilt, which blocks the flow of water through the plant's stems. Cucumbers are especially susceptible to bacterial wilt, for which there is no remedy. Infected plants will wilt and die within days. A few cucumber beetles in the patch isn't a guarantee of bacterial wilt. The beetle must first pick up the disease bacterium, usually from weeds that may

Grow them up instead of out. Pickler vines have tendrils, making them perfect for training up a trellis or fence.

A layer of row cover helps hide cucumbers. The covering will thwart the cucumber beetle, but it must be removed for pollination.

not show symptoms of the disease. But the risk of wilt is always there if the cucumber beetle is present.

Young plants are the most susceptible to damage from the striped cucumber beetle. Once a plant has developed at least three pairs of true leaves, it can tolerate considerable damage to its foliage without reducing its yield. You can protect young plants from cucumber beetles with a row cover, but eventually it must be removed to let bees and other insects pollinate the flowers. My defense against beetles and bacterial wilt is to plant cucumbers several times a year. If the plants are protected until they need pollination, chances are they will produce a decent crop before the wilt strikes—if it strikes at all. Planting successive crops a few weeks apart assures me of fresh cucumbers all season long, even if the beetles do in one or more of the plantings.

To be sure I get the most from each planting, I like to plant gynoecious varieties, like 'Calypso' and 'Royal'. Cucumbers are naturally monoecious, which means that they have male and female flowers on the same plant. Gynoecious varieties produce mostly female flowers, which makes them capable of producing nearly twice the amount of fruit as monoecious varieties because only female flowers produce fruit.

You will need a few male flowers to provide pollen. Seed companies take care of this by including in the packet a few seeds of a monoecious variety, which are usually dyed a vivid color so you can be sure to plant a few along with your gynoecious cucumbers. There's another class of cucumbers: parthenocarpic varieties, which require no pollination and produce seedless fruit. Most of the

get flabby in the middle when allowed to get too big. No varieties are particularly long-lived in the fridge. They respire through their skins and get wrinkly—hence, the supermarket cuke with its protective coat of wax or shrink-wrap. A week or so is the top storage time.

Compact varieties grow fast in almost any amount of space, given enough water and sunlight and a healthy soil.

available parthenocarpic cucumbers are slicers, but a pickler variety called 'Cool Breeze' is both parthenocarpic and burpless.

CUCUMBERS WANT WARM, TENDER SOIL

Picklers are warm-weather plants and will sprout readily if sown directly in warm soil. You can gain a little time on the season by starting the plants indoors, but be forewarned that cucumbers, like all cucurbits, resent having their roots disturbed. If you choose to use seedlings rather than seeds, start them in peat pots no sooner than three weeks before you intend to plant them outdoors, and transplant carefully to avoid root damage.

Sow two or three seeds together—in the ground or in a peat pot—and let the young plants grow up together. There's no need to thin them out. Cucumbers like a light, fertile soil. If your garden has heavy clay soil, lighten it with compost or peat before attempting cucumbers. Good compost also will provide the steady supply of nutrients that cucumbers need. If you use commercial, granulated fertilizer, mix a generous handful into the soil at planting and side-dress at least once during the season.

Adequate moisture is critical. Cucumbers need a deep soaking once a week, at a minimum. Mulching is a good idea, too. It will help prevent the soil from drying out between waterings, and it will keep weeds down. This is important for cucumbers, because pulling weeds by hand or cultivating with a hoe might damage those sensitive roots.

Start harvesting pickler cucumbers when they are 2 to 3 inches long but no more than 5 inches long. Picklers

4

ROOT VEGGIES

GO BEYOND
BASIC BEETS

Fresh beets are so much more than the canned, pickled variety you grew up eating—and avoiding. So get rid of your preconceived notions and give this spectacular vegetable a try in your garden. With gardener Joe Queirolo's tips, they're so easy to grow, you'll want to explore the wide diversity they offer.

I SUPPOSE BEETS MIGHT BE APPRECIATED MORE IF THEY HUNG from trees like apples instead of spending their lives in the soil. Glistening in the sunlight in colors ranging from magenta to gold to white, they might then be described as "sweet" and "bright" and "airy." As it is, dwelling underground and showing up in many of our memories as canned red balls or corrugated slices from a jar, they've developed an undeserved reputation as earthy and dull. Perhaps it's time to bring the many virtues of beets out into the light.

Beets can be easy and satisfying to grow if you prepare the soil well, fertilize carefully, sow the seed lavishly, and thin them conscientiously. Beetroots vary in shape and color from the small, globular, radish-colored 'Chioggia' to the lumpy, industrial-strength white sugar beet. Their flesh can be the prototypical blood red, golden, white, or red-and-white-ringed. All of them are sweet, and all can play colorful roles in the kitchen. The varied and versatile beet well deserves a spot in any garden.

Beets are jewels from the garden. Although they come in a range of sparkling colors, all beets have a flavor that is sweet and rich.

you see alternating rings of red and white (see the photo at left). I've heard it called the "target beet," and if you grate it, you get candy stripes. When it's cooked, the rings fade into one another and take on the color of a sunset. I also occasionally grow long, cylindrical red beets called 'Cylindra' (syn. 'Formanova'), which give you uniformly colored slices.

GIVE THEM LOTS OF NITROGEN AND PROPER SPACE

I worked a long time to get consistently good beets. Some years, I'd get a crop of large, smooth, round ones with lush greens. Other years, I'd get a scraggly crop of babies that refused to grow up. I eventually realized that those that didn't grow well had been struggling with soil depleted by a preceding heavy-feeding crop, like broccoli.

Along with loose soil, which will allow them to grow uniformly, beets need plenty of nitrogen. Feed them well, by adding well-composted manure to loosen the soil and about 3 pounds of seed meal (6-1-1) per 100 square feet. This will improve the soil texture and raise the nitrogen levels. Once you've done this, rake the bed smooth.

To sow beet seeds, dent the soil surface with your fingers every 3 inches in an offset pattern. Drop a couple of seeds in each shallow depression (more for 'Golden' beets, which don't germinate well), cover them with soil, and sift compost over the entire planting bed. Be sure to water the bed and keep it moist until the seedlings emerge in about a week. Sometimes, if I'm in a desperate hurry or my back is tired, I broadcast the seed, chop it in with a rake, and sift compost over the surface. Thinning becomes a bit more tedious this way and the spacing is uneven, but it is quick.

THINNING INCREASES THE HARVEST

The corky-looking beet seed you plant is actually a cluster of up to six individual seeds (see the top photo on the facing page). This means that, after the seedlings emerge, you'll have to thin them down to one if you want well-developed beets. If you wait to thin until the leaves are several inches long, you can use the thinnings—some with immature beets attached—to cook with in the kitchen. Leave the most vigorous-looking plant in each group and pull the rest (see the bottom photo on the facing page). Water after thinning to firm the loosened soil. Don't try to transplant the thinnings unless you're

ABOVE Grow a beet that's right on target. It's easy to see why 'Chioggia' is sometimes called the bull's-eye beet. Neither 'Chioggia' nor the golden beet bleeds its color when sliced open.

RIGHT They taste great but leave their mark. Traditional red beets are full of flavor, but their juices tend to stain everything they come in contact with.

DIFFERENT KINDS GIVE YOU DIFFERENT FLAVORS

I grow beets of many shapes and colors, and I harvest them at various stages, depending on how they'll be used. Although I do have a few standard red beets in the garden, I prefer to grow varieties that don't bleed when you cut them. These are useful when you want beet flavor and texture without turning everything red.

The ivory-colored variety called 'Detroit White' is very sweet, almost like a sugar beet. The 'Golden' beet has a fuller but less sweet flavor than 'Detroit White' and cooks up to a deep orange-red. My favorite, though, is 'Chioggia', named after a city on Italy's Adriatic coast. The skin is bright magenta, like a radish. When you slice it crosswise,

LEFT Beet seeds look weird for a reason. Each cluster is actually several seeds fused together. This helps improve beet seeds' naturally low germination rate.

ABOVE Thinning isn't optional if you want nicely shaped roots. Pull out all but one plant from every seed cluster, holding onto the beet you're leaving behind to keep it from being dislodged, too.

growing them only for the leaves; transplanted beetroots end up rough, gnarly, and twisted. Continue to keep the soil moist but not saturated.

I sow a succession of beets every few weeks beginning in the spring and ending in the fall, making sure they are adequately watered during the warm days of summer. You can harvest beets at any size. I usually harvest about 60 days after seeding by poking around in the soil and pulling those that are 2 inches or larger in diameter.

TRY BEET GREENS AND FALL CROPS

Although the leaves of all beets are fine to eat, there are a few varieties that I grow especially for their unique and

BEET BASICS

- Prepare a seed bed by working in compost and fertilizer. Smooth with a rake, then make shallow indentations 3 inches apart.

- Plant beets every three to four weeks from spring into fall for multiple harvests.

- Beet seeds are conglomerates—clusters of multiple seeds. After they germinate, pull out all but one seedling.

- Harvest when the beetroots are about 2 inches across.

tasty foliage. 'Lutz Green Leaf' (syn. 'Winter Keeper') has abundant, pale green leaves that approach the size of chard and taste delicious. 'Bull's Blood' has dark maroon, almost purple, leaves. It looks good in the garden, and you can pick the smaller leaves all season to add color to a salad. Larger leaves are better cooked, more tender, and sweeter than chard, although not as tender as spinach. 'MacGregor's Favorite' has elongated, iridescent leaves that vary from dark red to green with red veins. I've found that if I only lightly harvest the tops of these leaf beets, I can still get some massive roots.

I often sow a few overwintering beets in midsummer and let them size up during the fall. When cold weather comes, they can be left in the ground in mild zones, heavily mulched in moderate areas, or lifted out of the ground in cooler climates. With the leaves twisted off, they'll keep for a long time in the refrigerator. My favorite beet for later in the season is 'Lutz Green Leaf'. Its root is deep red, is 4 to 5 inches across, and keeps well.

I find a great deal of pleasure in growing beets. I like the rugged texture of the seeds; they look battered, scarred, and tough. I like preparing the smooth seed bed. Above all, I like to harvest a few beets of each variety and take them to the faucet to wash off the soil. As the colors appear under the running water, they look like jewels to me. And at that moment, with my hands full of nothing more than humble beets, I feel rich beyond measure.

SWEET, CRUNCHY
CARROTS

Farm manager Leonard Diggs shows you how consistent moisture and fertile soil assure great-tasting carrots.

YOU MIGHT HAVE HEARD THAT IF YOU WANT TO GROW GREAT carrots, you need fine, sandy soil that is free of clods and rocks—soil you can sink your arm into up to your elbow. Well, that's just great, but for most soils, it's a struggle to get your finger in up to the first joint.

There are advantages to inheriting perfect soil, but soils heavy with clay and full of pebbles, small sticks, and bits of organic matter don't have to be obstacles to successful carrot growing. Some soil amendment and preparation are necessary to grow great-tasting carrots. But sticking to a strict watering schedule, especially when carrot seeds are germinating, is equally important.

Most of the carrots you see in the supermarket are an 8- to 10-inch-long variety called 'Imperator'. Having these long orange icicles as examples of what carrots are supposed to look like fosters the myth that only perfectly straight carrots are acceptable. If you harvest your carrots when they are young and tender, their sweet taste will override any peculiarities in their shape.

Carrots aren't as finicky as you might think. With a little work up front, you'll be pulling up harvests by the handful.

Sow the seed carefully into neat rows. Space is important with carrots, so combine the seed with sand (right) for even distribution, and be sure that there's room between rows (above) to make weeding easier.

COMPOST ENHANCES SOIL TEXTURE AND FERTILITY

One of the first gardening lessons I learned was not to turn over your soil unless you are planning to add something to it. My "something" of choice is compost. Especially if your soil is heavy and full of clay, turning half an inch of compost into your soil is a good way to improve the growth of your carrots. Compost also loosens the soil, making it easier for carrots to push through. The organic matter feeds micro-organisms, too, helping make nutrients available to the roots. Clods of soil should be broken up and the compost thoroughly mixed in to a depth of 5 to 7 inches.

Compost is a slow-release fertilizer. It can take as long as three years for the soil to break down the compost so that the nutrients are available to plants. If you haven't added compost to your bed for the past two years, you may want to amend the bed with fertilizers that will feed the carrots sooner than compost. I prefer a combination of fish meal, kelp meal, and gypsum. Follow the instructions on the bags as to how much to use.

It's important to mix the fertilizer thoroughly into the soil. A concentrated band of powdered fertilizer in the first few inches of topsoil can cause problems. When the growing carrot tips hit the concentrated fertilizer, the carrots are liable to develop side shoots or split in two. It's also likely that these carrots won't taste very good.

SAND HELPS YOU SOW

Carrot seeds are tiny and half-moon shaped; a pinch will give you almost 20 seeds. The ideal distance to plant carrot seeds is 1 inch apart—any closer and you'll need to thin the seedlings after they sprout. Because the seeds are so minuscule, it's difficult to space them accurately. I mix carrot seed with coarse-grain sand, about 60 percent sand to 40 percent seed. Adding sand increases the volume of

CARROT BASICS

- Thoroughly mix compost into the top 5 to 7 inches of soil.

- Mix the tiny seeds with coarse sand to help you plant them evenly.

- Sow the seeds in rows 5 to 6 inches apart, or broadcast them over weed-free beds.

- After sowing, cover the seed with ½ inch of soil.

- Water the germinating seeds thoroughly in the morning and again in the evening.

- Reduce watering to once a day when the tops reach 1 inch high.

Harvesting is a snap with a digging fork. Push the fork into the soil to the side of the carrots. Grab the carrot tops with one hand and push down on the fork handle with the other hand, causing the carrots to pop out of the ground.

RAINBOW CARROTS

When I decided to start growing them, I couldn't resist trying every color I could get seeds for. The following are my favorites.

- 'Amarillo': As you can probably guess by the name, this is a yellow carrot that has a sweet flavor and is juicy.

- 'Atomic Red': This one you need to see to believe. The red flesh has a fresh flavor and loads of lycopene, which is said to help prevent some types of cancer.

- 'Cosmic Purple': A favorite at farmers' markets, this cool carrot is purple on the outside and has shades of orange and yellow on the inside. The taste is spicy and sweet.

- 'Lunar White': Mild tasting yet delicious, this carrot is rarely available at markets, so it's a real treat to grow your own.

- 'Danvers 126 Half Long': This is, by far, my favorite-tasting, plain old orange carrot. I like growing this variety because it was developed in Danvers, Massachusetts, not far from where I live. —PATTI MORENO, MASS. GARDENER

material that you're working with. This makes it easier to control the seed spacing as you let a thin stream of sand and seed pour from your hand (see the right photo on the facing page).

I like to plant carrot seeds ½ inch deep in rows 5 to 6 inches apart. Planting in defined rows will allow you to see and remove the weeds much more easily (see the left photo on the facing page). Carrots germinate slowly, usually taking 8 to 17 days. Get rid of any weed seedlings you find before the carrots start to come up. Hand pulling and hoeing are my first lines of defense. I like to remove the weeds when they're small, before they turn into large trees with deep, spreading roots.

WATER DEEPLY AND ROTATE YEARLY

If you want your carrot seeds to germinate and to continue to do well as young seedlings, you have to water them adequately. Depending on your soil type, it can take a solid five minutes or more, once in the morning and once in the evening, to get the water to percolate deep enough to soak your seeds. My favorite way of watering is to connect my garden timer to a sprinkler or soaker hose. The $^1/_2$ inch of soil you've put over your seeds helps prevent the seeds from drying out before germination and from being heaved up out of the ground when the soil heats up.

When the carrot tops have grown an inch above the soil line, cut your watering back to once a day. When the carrots' roots are 3 to 4 inches long (you'll have to dig up

a few baby carrots to check the size), cut your watering back to once every other day. Carrots do not grow well if the soil and air are too hot or too cold. The optimal temperature is between 60°F and 84°F. Planting carrots every two to three weeks will ensure a ready supply of tender roots. When it is time to harvest these golden nuggets, I stick my digging fork into the ground to the sides of the carrots. I pull the handle back, which lifts and frees the carrots (see the photo above). I can then pull them from the soil without breaking their tops off.

If you grow carrots in the same area season after season, insects and disease-causing organisms can build up in the soil and become serious problems. Try not to return your carrots to the same bed for at least three seasons—five is even better—to ensure a bountiful harvest.

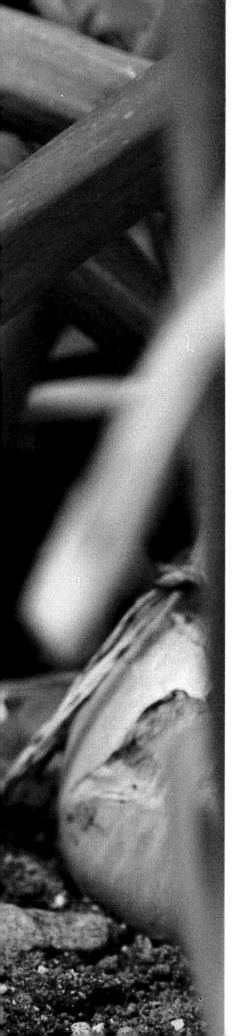

ONIONS
FROM SEED

This kitchen staple can be so much more than what you find at the grocery store. Starting onions from seed allows you to pick the best kinds for flavor, color, and storage. Gardener Leslie A. Clapp tells you what you need to succeed.

LIKE MOST GARDENERS, I STARTED OUT GROWING ONIONS FROM sets, which are small, immature onion bulbs. They were easy to grow, and I soon wanted to expand my varietal horizons. But I found that, with onion sets, my choices were limited. So I turned to seeds. Growing from seed let me pick varieties to suit my own needs or whims—such as the desire for an early-season sweet onion or a late-season keeper. And my choice of colors is wide, ranging from dashing purple to pure white and numerous shades of yellow. Shapes and sizes vary, too, from the bottle-shaped 'Italian Red Torpedo' to the plump perfection of 'Ailsa Craig' (see the photo at left).

Most onion experts agree that, diversity aside, onions grown from seed perform better than those grown from sets. They are less prone to disease, store better, and bulb up faster. I was convinced after my first year of growing onions from seed. The rewards were clear: I had a bin full of one of the most essential vegetables there is.

A perfect bulb is easier to grow than you might think. As the onion matures, brush soil away from its base so that it perches on top of the ground. Here, the roots of 'Ailsa Craig' firmly anchor it to the soil.

BELOW Sow, separate, then transplant. Onions do best when they are started in flats that are topped off with vermiculite.

ABOVE When the seedlings are 5 to 6 inches tall, it's time to transplant them into individual cells. Gently separate the roots of the seedlings from each other, holding each seedling by the green tops.

LEFT Don't forget to leave some room to grow. Transplant seedlings into loose, fertile loam, spacing them about 6 inches apart.

If short-day onions are grown in the North, they will bulb too early, then languish and never grow to a good size. On the other hand, if long-day onions are grown in the South, they'll produce lots of leaves but no respectable bulbs.

KNOW THE DIFFERENCE IN DAY LENGTHS

Onions need a long growing season, so place your seed orders early to get a head start. When choosing seed, make sure to order types suited to your climate and zone. Onion varieties differ in the length of daylight and the temperature required to make a bulb. Short-day types are ideal for the South, where they grow through the cool southern fall and winter months. They are triggered to bulb by the 12 hours of sunlight that comes with the return of warm, early summer weather.

Long-day onions are best grown in the North, where the summer-daylight period is longer. These onions require at least 14 hours of light to bulb up. The plant grows foliage in cool spring weather, then forms bulbs during warm summer weather, triggered by the long days.

START SEEDS IN FLATS

Lingering cold temperatures and soggy ground keep me out of the garden most years until mid-May. So I must start my seeds inside at least two months before the last frost or there won't be quality bulbs at harvest, especially because I grow the large, sweet Spanish types.

I sow seeds in flats filled with soilless potting mix and then cover them with a thin layer of vermiculite (see the top left photo above). I put a plastic top over the flats with to keep in moisture, and place the flats on the heated floor of a sunroom. Onions germinate in about a week at around 70°F. Once their stringlike tops poke through the soil, I change the growing conditions. I remove the plastic top and move the flats to my cool attic, where they're placed under fluorescent lights. I keep the lights

If you know your onions, your kitchen and pantry can be well stocked with great varieties.

'AILSA CRAIG': A huge, round, mild, snow white onion with straw yellow skin. Matures well in northern gardens. Stores into late fall. Matures in 110 days.

'CANDY': The big-boy onion, averaging 5 pounds. Crisp and sweet. Great to use for stuffing or onion rings. Short-term storage. Matures in 85 days.

'COPRA': An early onion with medium-size, blocky globe bulbs and dark yellow skin. Rock-hard bulb makes it unrivaled for storage. Also has the highest sugar content of the storage onions. Matures in 104 days.

'FIRST EDITION': A medium-size onion with pungent flavor. Good for storage. Matures in 105 days.

'KELSAE SWEET GIANT': Holds the Guinness World Record for the largest onion in the world, weighing in at more than 15 pounds. Long-day variety that matures in 110 days.

'RED BARON': A large, purple-red beauty. Also good for storage. Matures in 108 days.

'WHITE EBENEZER': A long-day onion well suited to northern gardens. Perfect for fresh eating and for pickling. Matures in 85 days.

Onions can be beautiful. When grown in mixed edible beds (right), onions' tall green tops and colorful bulbs (below) are as eye-catching as they are mouthwatering.

just above the leaves, adjusting them as the plants grow. I feed the seedlings with a water-soluble fertilizer at half strength every other time I water, being careful not to keep them too wet. Finally, I thin them to one every ¼ inch or so.

I transplant the onions into six-packs when the leaves are 5 to 6 inches tall, usually by mid-March. Because onion seedlings are fragile, this job is somewhat tedious. Some people skip this step by going from flats directly to the garden, but by allowing each one its own growing space, I give my onions the best possible chance for root development.

I carefully overturn the flat to expose the seedlings' roots. Handling the plants by the leaves, I gently tug to separate the roots of individual plants. I then tuck each plant into its new cell without damaging the long, threadlike roots. Using scissors, I snip the leaves back to about 4 inches long to keep the plant from being too top-heavy and to give more nutrients to the roots instead of the leaves. I continue watering with half-strength soluble fertilizer and keep the seedlings under grow lights. If your weather allows, you could move your transplants to a cold frame; onions are cold-hardy plants and can stand chilly temperatures. Here in Maine, I usually wait until mid-April to put them in my cold frames.

GET THEM INTO THE GROUND EARLY

If you are fortunate enough to have a garden you can work early in the season, you may opt to seed your onions directly in the ground. I generally set out my transplants (and sets, if I have any) in mid-May, when they are about half the size of a pencil. Whether growing from seed, set, or transplant, onions need soil that is high in organic matter and well drained. Onions prefer fertile, loose loam with a pH of 6 to 6.5. I usually work in an organic fertilizer, such as North Country Organics's Pro-Gro 5-3-4.

I transplant the seedlings ½ inch deep, 4 to 6 inches apart. If the mature bulb is large, I give it 6 inches; if smaller, 4 inches is adequate (see the bottom photo on p. 106). Once they're in the ground, I cut the top-heavy leaves back to 6 inches long. I plant some varieties closer and thin them as summer progresses. I use thinned onions in salads and cooking.

To conserve space, I plant in double or triple rows 6 inches apart, with 1 to 2 feet between the rows. Planting in rows, as opposed to beds, cuts down on maintenance because rows are easier to weed. I keep onions well weeded to avoid competition for light, water, and nutrients. And I pull weeds by hand to avoid damaging the shallow onion roots.

Water and nutrients are an important part of onion growing. The soil surface should be evenly moist. I give onion plants at least 1 inch of water a week, and make

A FOOLPROOF CURING SYSTEM

One of the biggest mistakes gardeners make is leaving their onions in the ground too long before harvesting. This invites damage that will result in a shorter shelf life. I harvest when the bulbs have sized up and the tops are browning. On a clear, sunny day, pull onions gently from the ground. Do not peel them or rinse them with water, because this will also shorten their storage life.

I've learned to allow at least a month for post-harvest curing (drying and healing of wounds). I lay my onions out on window screens propped up on sawhorses, out of direct sun, in a well-ventilated spot. Bulbs should be spaced fairly wide apart to allow good air circulation; I also use a fan to help move the air around. Turn the onions over periodically, and remove spoiled ones. Once the onion foliage has withered, I cut off the tops (leaving an inch or so) and trim the roots. I then give the

bulbs a gentle brushing and remove some of the outer layers of skin. The onions that look iffy go to the kitchen for immediate use; the others can be hung up in mesh bags for long-term storage.
—AMY GOLDMAN, N.Y. GARDENER

sure there is a constant supply of moisture during the bulb-enlarging stage. If it's too dry and plants are grown under stress, the bulbs will be smaller and have a stronger flavor. If you have a dry season, consider mulching onions with grass clippings or leaves. Be sure to keep the mulch away from bulbs to avoid disease and rot.

Onions are heavy feeders, so besides the initial feeding at planting time, they'll benefit from fertilizer or a side-dressing of manure when the bulbs begin to swell. If you don't give onions adequate potassium, their necks will thicken and the bulbs won't store well. As the onions start to mature, ease up on water and fertilizer to encourage dormancy.

HARVEST, CURE, AND STORE

As the onion matures, pull the soil away from most of the bulb so that only the roots and the lowest part of the bulb are in contact with the dirt. It will look as if the onion is sitting on top of the soil, as it should (see the photo on p. 104). This will aid in the drying process by keeping

moist soil away from the papery skins. To ensure healthy bulbs, rotate the crop yearly.

If onion maggots are a problem in your area, don't plant too early in the spring, and consider using row covers to discourage the egg-laying flies. When all is said and done, onions are an easy addition to the garden, and they are virtually pest- and disease-free.

As the end of August rolls around, you should see signs that harvest time is near. At full maturity, the plants go dormant: The inner leaves stop producing blades, and the hollow-centered neck weakens, causing the tops to bend over. It is important to let the plants go dormant before harvesting, or they won't store well.

During a dry spell, pull the bulbs after the tops have withered and place them in a warm, dry, airy location out of direct sun and out of contact with moist soil. Onions can be stored in a traditional onion bag or in a shallow box with newspaper dividing the bulbs. Or you can place an onion in a pair of panty hose and tie a knot above the onion; tie knots between each additional bulb. When you're ready to use a bulb, cut below the knot and proceed to the kitchen.

GROWING
NEW POTATOES

Bigger might seem better with potatoes, but harvesting your spuds when they're young gets you better flavor. Organic gardener Carrie Chalmers tells you all you need to know to get a variety of yummy new potatoes.

WE WOULD HAND-DIG THE FIRST HARVEST OF NEW POTATOES near the end of June at the vegetable farm where I used to work on Martha's Vineyard. Lifting a healthy green plant from the soil to reveal clusters of small red potatoes clinging to the roots was as thrilling to me as peeking into a bird's nest and finding a clutch of tiny eggs.

Customers flocked to the farm stand in search of vegetables for the traditional Fourth of July meal of new potatoes, fresh peas, and salmon with dill. The new potatoes were displayed clean and still wet. With their jewel-like red skins, they were often mistaken for radishes.

New potatoes add not only subtle flavor but also beautiful colors to any dish.

FINGERLING
Low in starch. Use roasted, steamed, or boiled.

RED SKINNED
Low in starch. Use in potato salads and gratins, or fried.

YUKON GOLD
Medium starch. Use baked or mashed or in soups.

HARVESTING EARLY HAS MANY ADVANTAGES

New potatoes are simply immature spuds, sized somewhere between a marble and a golf ball. Fragile skinned and moist, they are best cooked in their jackets soon after digging. Like the first asparagus of spring or the first raspberries of summer, new potatoes are a luxury of the garden. Growing unusual varieties and harvesting them during the summer can expand the potato lover's choices beyond the plastic-bagged whites and dusty reds of the supermarket shelves.

If you have a small garden, harvesting potatoes early can open up valuable space as early as July for other vegetables, like carrots, beans, lettuce, and radishes. Your overall yield of potatoes will be smaller when you harvest them young, but you can replant in the same space to enjoy a great selection of vegetables in late summer.

A midsummer harvest can also end insect worries early. Anyone who has grown potatoes knows the Colorado potato beetle (see the top sidebar on the facing page).

Harvesting the whole plant for new potatoes reduces the length of time you'll have to patrol your potato patch.

Different varieties of potatoes have varying resistance to disease and to less-than-perfect climates. Where one type might not thrive, another type might be more adaptable. By experimenting, you can discover varieties suited to your soil and microclimate. And many seed-potato companies will sell you small amounts of several varieties in an experimenter's pack.

CHOOSE A FLAVORFUL VARIETY

At the farm stand on Martha's Vineyard, the potatoes our customers bought were either 'Red Norland' or 'Dark Red Norland'. Both varieties have red skin and moist white flesh. 'Red Norland' is ready to eat soon after the plants blossom, about 50 days after planting, making them the earliest variety to harvest.

Yukon Gold potatoes have thin, golden skin and creamy yellow flesh. They are a good choice for new potatoes, with wonderful flavor and texture for cooking and smooth,

uniform skins. It is an early maturing variety, yielding gold nuggets by early to mid-July. 'Rose Gold' is the red-skinned counterpart to Yukon Gold. With lovely, translucent pink skin, waxy yellow flesh, and good disease resistance, it makes an appealing new potato, ready to harvest about two weeks later than Yukon Gold.

Fingerlings are elongated, finger-size tubers with exquisite flavor and texture. My father began growing fingerlings at the suggestion of a friend who had grown up in France, where his mother had raised fingerlings. The flesh is yellow, the skin is tender, and the texture is smooth and dense.

'Russian Banana', a popular fingerling, has golden skin and is late to mature. While it is not ideal as a very early new potato because of its long growing period—about 70 days for new potatoes—it is worth growing for a later harvest of exceptionally tasty potatoes. By August, there should be a good supply of small to medium fingerlings, and luckily, the quality is just as good when they grow to maturity.

'Rose Finn Apple' is a pink-skinned counterpart to the 'Russian Banana'. It's ready to eat about 10 days earlier than 'Russian Banana'. It, too, has a wonderful flavor, although it tends to be more irregularly shaped than its golden counterpart.

I recently started growing two unusual varieties, 'Cranberry Red' and 'All Blue'. Both varieties are remarkable for their brightly colored flesh. 'Cranberry Red' has a red skin and a moist, light red flesh. 'All Blue' has blue flesh. It boasts excellent flavor, is harvested slightly later than 'Cranberry Red', and produces a good yield of small tubers.

LOCATE THE EYES, DIG THE HOLES, THEN HILL THEM UP

Potatoes are grown not by planting seeds but, rather, by planting an actual piece of a potato. You've probably seen tubelike sprouts growing from a potato you've had around for a while. The sprouts are growing from the potato's "eyes," which are dormant buds.

You might be tempted to plant a supermarket potato in the ground and expect it to grow. But most potatoes

Be sure there are two eyes per piece. All but the tiniest seed potatoes should be cut into chunks that have at least two growing sprouts each.

ABOVE Plant them cut side down. Before placing the spuds into their planting holes, put in a scoop of compost.

LEFT Hilling has a few advantages. It increases your crop and prevents sunlight from reaching the tubers and turning them green.

sold in grocery stores are treated with a sprout inhibitor that takes a long time to become inactive. Also, and more important, soil-borne diseases, harmless to humans but potentially devastating for a potato plant, can be carried by potatoes. It's safest to buy seed potatoes that are certified to be disease-free.

Prior to planting, I like to cut in half all the seed potatoes that are larger than a lime. I also halve fingerlings larger than my thumb. But before you cut a potato in half, take a look at it, and figure out the best way to make the cut so that each piece will have at least two eyes. Large potatoes with numerous eyes can be cut into three pieces. Take care

not to break off any of the eyes; if they do snap off, the eye will most likely sprout again, but it will take longer before the new sprout breaks ground. I usually cut the seed just before I plant it, waiting until the soil reaches 50°F. Seed potatoes can rot or take forever to sprout if they're planted in ground that is too wet or too cool.

Potatoes grow easily in well-drained, fertile soil that has the proper balance of nutrients. Too much nitrogen and insufficient phosphorus will cause the leaves to grow vigorously at the expense of the tubers. Aged manure, compost, and leaf mold are all excellent organic amendments to mix into your soil to create the rich, nutrient-balanced medium that potatoes thrive in. I never add lime where I'm going to plant potatoes because a slightly acidic soil will help inhibit growth of the scab organism.

Common practice when growing potatoes to maturity is to plant them in 6-inch-deep holes, with the seed potatoes spaced about a foot apart. But if you plan to harvest new potatoes, you can get away with planting them closer—6 to 8 inches apart. By crowding the plants, the tubers do not have room to grow as quickly into larger spuds.

To plant, I add about half a shovelful of compost and place the seed potato, cut side down, on top of the compost. I then cover each seed with another 2 to 3 inches of compost.

Shallow planting allows the soil around the seed to warm quickly, encouraging faster sprouting. As the plant grows and the tubers start to form, they must be protected from sunlight to keep them from becoming green. The solanine in green potatoes can turn them bitter and mildly toxic.

When the plants get 4 to 6 inches tall, cover them so that only a couple of inches of leaves show above the soil, a process called hilling. Use a hoe or your hands to mound the soil around the plant. If you're growing early varieties, one hilling will be enough, but with later types, a second hilling in two to three weeks is a good idea. Again, mound the soil to cover some of the lower leaves.

Be sure to water the plants regularly and thoroughly. This is particularly important when the plants begin to develop tubers. A dry spell followed by heavy watering causes irregular growth spurts, encourages scab, and can result in cracked or odd-shaped tubers.

THERE'S ALWAYS SPACE FOR SPUDS

As an urban gardener with an 8-foot-long balcony as my backyard, I thought that I would never be able to grow potatoes. But where there's a will, there's a way. Last year, I successfully grew potatoes in a can—a kitchen garbage pail, to be precise. Here's how you can do it, too. —Brandi Spade, Penn. gardener

1. Select a clean plastic container that has a depth of at least 2 feet. Drill several drainage holes in the bottom, and fill it 5 inches from the top with potting mix.

2. Press one or two potato starts about 6 inches into the soil with the eyes facing toward the sun. Cover the starts with soil. As the foliage starts to emerge, continue mounding soil around the plants (leaving some of the leaves exposed).

3. Keep the soil moist (but not soggy to prevent rot) as the plants grow throughout the season. Apply an organic fertilizer once, after the plants are a few inches high. When the plant is done flowering, you can harvest small baby potatoes, or wait until the plant dies back completely if you want larger tubers.

ABOVE Flowering often means it's time to harvest. Not all plants will blossom, though, so be sure to check the size of the tubers seven weeks after planting.

RIGHT Don't be afraid to pull them out. Once you've decided it's time to harvest, use a shovel to help unearth the entire plant.

AVOID PESTS FOR A SUCCESSFUL HARVEST

Planting seed potatoes certified to be free of diseases is the first way to ensure a good crop of new potatoes. Changing the piece of ground each year in which you grow potatoes also helps control insects and diseases. But the potato's worst enemy, the Colorado potato beetle, is an uninvited guest in almost every garden (see the sidebar on p. 113). Keeping your healthy plants from being devoured by these critters requires considerable diligence.

I handpick the adult beetles as they emerge from their underground winter hideouts, and I check under leaves for their orange eggs. Crushing the egg masses will keep them from hatching into ravening larvae, which then turn into adults.

Lightweight floating row covers are great for controlling potato bugs. After planting the seed, cover your rows with thin polyester fabric. The edges should be sealed thoroughly by shoveling small amounts of soil along the entire length of the fabric. When the adult Colorado potato beetles emerge from their winter home in the vegetation along the edge of your garden, they'll find a barrier between them and your plants. The cover should stay on as long as possible, coming off when the weather is hot or when the plants outgrow the cover. Contending with bugs is much easier for a large, healthy plant than it is for a young plant just getting established.

The stage at which Colorado potato beetles do the most damage is after the eggs hatch into larvae. Larvae are easily identifiable in this soft-bodied stage by their reddish color and humped back and by the two rows of

Don't scrub the spuds. New potatoes have thin, delicate skins and don't need to be peeled before eating, so wash them gently.

black dots down each side. The larvae feed on the potato leaves, and they can quickly defoliate entire plantings. You can kill the larvae by spraying on a solution of *Bacillus thuringiensis* (Bt) var. *san diego*. This microbe is not harmful to people or to beneficial insects, and it leaves no residue. It is effective only on larvae less than ¼ inch long. Bt is available through catalogs that offer organic-gardening supplies and at many garden centers.

Blossoming potato plants are sometimes a good indication that new potatoes are ready to harvest. But not all potato plants blossom. So about seven weeks after the plants break ground, I uncover the sides of the mound to check on the size of the tubers. If they are not ready, I pack the soil back around the roots and wait a while.

How you harvest your potatoes is determined by how you are going to eat them. If you are going to eat all your potatoes when they're new, it's easiest to uproot the whole plant.

When I harvest the entire plant, I use a shovel and dig straight down a good foot away from the middle of the plant to avoid slicing into any of the tubers. Using one hand to pull the plant and the other to pry it out with the shovel, I lift up the plant gently. Most of the potatoes will hang off the roots. Be sure to dig around with your hands to rescue any stragglers that may have stayed in the ground.

But if you just want to poach a few small potatoes from each plant, use your hands to trespass in the soil, feeling around with your fingers for the little potatoes. You should pack the soil back around the disturbed roots and water the plant well. The skin of new potatoes is fragile, and it is easily scraped. So wash the potatoes gently in cool water, then cook and serve them as soon as you can.

RADISHES
FOR ALL SEASONS

For a peppery crunch, these fast-growing veggies are hard to beat. Market gardener Cynthia Hizer shares her secrets to fresh radishes practically year-round.

THE FIRST TIME I TOOK RADISHES SERIOUSLY WAS AT A DINNER party several years ago. I was assisting the executive chef at the Georgia Governor's Mansion in Atlanta. The day of the party, he filled me in on the menu; it started with a platter of fresh radishes.

I hadn't seen in a long time anyone put radishes out for noshing, and they certainly didn't fit in with my idea of a state dinner. So I wasn't prepared for the tiny, perfect radishes the chef presented that night, fragrant with spring and sweetly spicy. He served them as a first course with sea salt and homemade butter and bread. They were a sensation, and I was converted.

Around the world, people celebrate the flavor and quirky nature of radishes. It is a custom for Chinese New Year to eat julienned radishes with dried apricots. In Oaxaca, Mexico, giant radishes are carved into animal shapes for a Christmas Eve festival known as "Night of the Radishes." And the British used to celebrate May 11 with a radish feast. Radishes' texture and jeweled colors should be enough to get them onto any gardener's and cook's must-have list.

There's a cornucopia of crunchiness to choose from. Radishes can vary in color, size, and spiciness. There are, in addition, spring varieties (pictured) and winter varieties, ensuring that there's a radish for every taste.

FAR LEFT Thin your plants for the best harvest. Radishes should be spaced 1½ inches apart. To eat the thinned greens in salads or stir-fries, be sure to pick them while they're still tender and hairless.

NEAR LEFT Twisted roots indicate poor soil. When long-rooted radishes (such as the daikon, pictured) hit a rock or heavy clay, irregular shapes are common.

MIX YOUR RADISH & CARROT SEEDS

Radish seeds are fairly large and easy to handle, while carrot seeds are tiny and difficult to evenly sow by hand. Carrots also need to be thinned for them to develop uniformly. But carrot sprouts look a lot like weeds, so figuring out what to pull and what to leave can be mind-numbing.

I solve these problems by evenly mixing my carrot and radish seeds. It's easy to tell the difference between the two sprouts after they germinate because they look vastly different— this also makes identifying weeds a snap. And because carrot seeds take a long time to germinate and grow but radishes are fairly quick to sprout and develop, the two are perfect companions. As the radish shoots mature, they can be pulled out and eaten, leaving behind nicely spaced carrots with more room to grow.

—ANNE DUNCAN, CONN. GARDENER

GIVE THEM LIGHT SOIL AND EVEN MOISTURE

Radishes are best when grown quickly in cool weather with constant moisture. There are spring and winter varieties. Spring radishes (see the photo on p. 118) are perfect for folks who want a crop in hand by the time the first robin sings. Most are ready in three to four weeks. One thing I especially appreciate about spring radishes is that they give the garden a mature look when it needs it the most. Winter radishes (see the photo on the facing page) are starchier, larger, and tend to be stronger in flavor. Sow them in late summer for fall and winter harvests. Winter radishes take six to eight weeks to mature. With tougher skins and denser flesh, they keep well for months, and they can be used at any size.

Being root vegetables, radishes are potassium users. A minimally fertile soil is adequate for most crops. Don't give the plants too much nitrogen, or you'll get more greens than root. A bit of composted manure will do for nitrogen, and some wood ashes or greensand in the fall will provide plenty of potassium. More important is having a light, airy soil.

You can plant radishes with other leaf crops, but they shouldn't follow cabbage because the two are susceptible

VARIETIES RANGE FROM CLASSIC TO ZANY

Spring radish varieties tend to be traditional in appearance (see the photo on p. 118). They come mostly in shades of red, pink, and white, and they are very tender—making them perfect for eating fresh.

Winter radishes come in a far more varied array of colors and textures. They can be long and pale, like the daikon variety, or round with rough, dark skin, like 'Black Spanish'. Because they are denser and more pungent than spring radishes, winter varieties are best when cooked like turnips or other root veggies.

'DAIKON'

'GREEN MEAT'

'RED MEAT'

'BLACK SPANISH'

to the same maladies. I sow radishes in the same part of my garden as my other root crops, because they all have the same nutritional needs.

SOW THEM EARLY, OR SOW THEM LATE

Radish lovers will find many varieties to try. Some options for spring include 'Champion', which likes cold weather and stays firm at maturity. 'Sora' handles warm weather better than other varieties. Globe shapes also come in white, red dipped in white, and shades of purple and pink. 'Easter Egg II' is a mix of red, white, and pastels.

There are also cylindrical spring radishes. The extra-mild 'French Breakfast' grows 3 to 4 inches long and is red on the top and white on the bottom. 'White Icicle' is an old-fashioned variety whose name is more descriptive of its appearance than of its flavor, which can be nicely pungent.

'Daikon' may be the most famous type of winter radish. Some cultivars of this mild, all-white radish can grow to 2 feet long in loose soils. Other delicious winter varieties I've grown include 'Red Meat' and 'Green Meat'. 'Black Spanish' radishes are round, with an ebony peel and peppery white flesh that sweetens in cooking. Its flesh

is denser and so takes longer to cook than other winter types. The black peel looks tough, but don't be too zealous in cleaning or you'll scrub it right off. Whether you choose spring or winter varieties, radishes provide a zesty option for the vegetable garden.

RADISH BASICS

- Plant seed in cold soil, as soon as it can be worked.

- Thin seedlings to 1½ inches apart.

- Keep soil evenly moist.

- To prevent flea beetles, cover beds with floating row covers right after planting.

- Hollow or oddly shaped radishes indicate stress from irregular watering, heavy soil, or excessively warm weather.

SQUASH

BEYOND
GREEN ZUCCHINI

Try some of these out-of-the-ordinary options for better flavor and a larger harvest. Gardener Sam Gittings shares his favorite varieties and his approach to harvesting the bounty from flower to fruit.

EVERY SUMMER, WHEN MY GARDEN REACHES FULL PRODUCTION, I tell myself, "Next year, plant fewer zucchini." Yet every spring, the urge to expand my garden, feed the homeless, and maybe cover the earth with zucchini overrides all common sense. Apparently, I am not alone in this compulsion. Each July, I place a small card in the front window of my dental office, warding off well-meaning gardener friends: "Thanks, but no more zucchini!"

Don't get me wrong. I love zucchini and summer squash, both in the garden and in the kitchen. They come in bright yellows, deep greens, and creamy whites, and in odd shapes—ridges, scallops, teardrops, and S curves. I continue to grow many varieties because I enjoy cooking with a mix of colors, textures, and shapes.

I have also learned that by harvesting squash at various stages throughout the season, I gain a wealth of exciting and delicious opportunities to make use of the abundance. I begin by harvesting flowers and baby fruit, both of which taste delicious and have many uses in the kitchen. During the height of summer, I harvest

Meet the members of this diverse family. If you think squash only comes in dark green or light yellow, think again. Varieties come in a range of colors, each with a unique flavor.

LEFT Pay attention to the form of 'Lungo Fiorentino'. If allowed to grow 7 to 9 inches long, defined ridges will appear and signal that the squash is ready to be picked.

TOP RIGHT Eat 'Ronde de Nice' as baby squash. Or leave them on the vine until fall, and they'll look like salmon-colored pumpkins.

BOTTOM RIGHT Count on 'Burpee's Golden Zucchini' to liven up your squash bed and give you supersweet flavor.

mature fruit, which I enjoy in soups, side dishes, and entrées. Finally, I leave some varieties to age on the plants. In fall, I harvest a colorful array of hard-shelled fruit to use as decorations at harvest parties, Halloween, and Thanksgiving.

SOW A SELECTION OF SUMMER SQUASH

One recent year, I limited myself to five summer squash varieties: 'Lungo Fiorentino', 'Ronde de Nice', 'Burpee's Golden Zucchini', 'Sunburst', and 'White Patty Pan'. ('White Patty Pan' is also known as 'White Bush Scallop' or 'Early White Bush Scallop'.)

'Lungo Fiorentino' (see the left photo above) is a dark green Italian zucchini with light green stripes and delightful ridges. I serve 'Lungo Fiorentino' cut into thick medallions to show off the ridges. The fruit has to grow 7 to 9 inches long for the ridges to be pronounced.

'Ronde de Nice' (see the top right photo above) produces smooth-textured, globe-shaped fruit. Although the globes look great as babies attached to the flower, I

grow 'Ronde de Nice' for what it becomes in fall. When I've had it with the garden and the gophers are taking their share, the 'Ronde de Nice' come alive. Their cheeks turn rosy and start to glow as the delicate light green skin of the young fruit hardens and matures to a beautiful salmon shade. I place the mature fruit on my front porch at Halloween, where they look like extraordinary pumpkins. I never carve them, though, because once the tough skin is broken, the flesh deteriorates quickly.

Because I'm a little tired of straight green zucchini, I grow 'Burpee's Golden Zucchini' instead (see the bottom right photo above). This variety produces slender, medium-long, cylindrical fruits that look a lot like green zucchini, except that they have glossy, bright golden skin.

'Sunburst' (see the left photo on the facing page) has the stunning yellow color of 'Burpee's Golden Zucchini' with the distinctive scalloped edges of a classic pattypan. It has a nutty flavor and tastes great when it's 3 to 4 inches wide. When the fruit are left to mature on the plants, their yellow skin hardens to a beautiful ocher color.

'White Patty Pan' (see the right photo on the facing page) is similar to 'Sunburst' but is creamy white in color.

LEFT 'Sunburst' squash plants produce like no other. Pattypan varieties like this are known to produce buckets of fruit in a given season.

ABOVE 'White Patty Pan' squash look like gourds but have a tender creaminess that is unique.

In the kitchen, I mix 'White Patty Pan' with green basil and red bell peppers to make colorful dishes. The fruits also make nice sculptural decorations when the shell has hardened. I have even taken them to galleries as objets d'art.

PLANT EXTRA SQUASH TO FILL IN GAPS

Summer squash is notoriously easy to grow. Unlike most gardeners, I plant mine in rows, not hills. Rows that are 5 to 6 feet apart are more convenient for weeding and for watering.

I prefer to plant seeds directly in the ground rather than to transplant seedlings. Mature, nursery-reared squash transplants—those with three or four leaves—have never done well for me. The shock of transplanting often stunts their growth all season. If I need to move squash plants around to fill in gaps, I always transplant seedlings just after the first true leaf opens.

I space my summer squash seeds a mere 14 inches apart in a row. This may seem close, but some competition

SQUASH BASICS

- Allow the soil to warm above 70°F before planting.
- Dig in lots of compost.
- Direct-sow to avoid transplant shock.
- Sow the seeds 14 inches apart in rows 4 to 5 feet apart.
- Keep young plants well weeded.
- Don't allow the soil to dry out.
- Pick fruit often to assure continual production.

ABOVE The reward of planting many varieties comes early. Young squash are sweet and tender, so the harvesting can start before they fully mature.

LEFT Pick early, and pick often. Harvesting usually begins 45 days after sowing. The more you pick, the more the squash vines will produce.

between plants is all right. And in my garden, the gophers can be counted on for their share of midseason thinning.

I plant two squash seeds per hole. If both seeds come up strong, I use the extra plant to fill in a gap. Last year, for instance, I filled the gaps left by a poor germination of 'Lungo Fiorentino' by moving in some leftover 'White Patty Pan' seedlings.

My summer squash grow so vigorously that they outpace most insect damage. I've never had a problem with vine borers, but I have had cucumber beetles nibble on the squash flowers. To control cucumber beetles, I spray the leaves with a thin slurry solution of diatomaceous earth and water (about 3 tablespoons per gallon). When the slurry solution dries, the leaves look whitewashed for five to six weeks and not particularly attractive, but the cucumber beetles stay away.

BEGIN YOUR HARVEST WITH THE BLOSSOMS

Because I don't listen to the sensible, analytical side of my brain, which tells me to plant fewer zucchini plants in spring, by August, I must listen to the creative side, which abhors waste and wants to make use of every squash that has grown. To me, each stage in the life of a squash is a culinary or decorative opportunity. I keep pace with the profusion of squash in my garden by beginning my harvest with the flowers.

I pick the flowers, male and female, in the early morning, when they are fully open; by afternoon, they've wilted and are difficult to stuff or use in cooking. I like to pick female flowers when their fruit is 1½ inches long.

Some people will tell you not to pick female flowers or else the plant will not produce fruit. I have found the opposite to be true. In an effort to reproduce itself, a squash plant robbed of female flowers will get angry and try even harder to produce fruit. If you regularly remove the fruit, the plant will kick into higher production than you ever dreamed possible. Still, you can't pick all the female flowers from all your plants or you won't get any mature squash.

Baby squash appear soon after the flowers bloom. Sometimes I pick them still attached to the flower. Other times, I harvest only the tiny fruit, which I either steam or eat raw.

Although I continue picking and cooking with flowers and babies throughout the summer, my attention

HELP POLLINATE YOUR SQUASH

Members of the squash family sometimes suffer from poor pollination. This problem has gotten worse in recent years because of the decline in the honeybee population and the loss of other natural insect pollinators. If you notice immature squash turning brown and rotting on the vine before reaching maturity, you may have a pollination issue. But don't despair; you can help the situation by pollinating your squash by hand. —CHIP TYNAN, MO. GARDENER

1. You'll need to determine the difference between male and female flowers on your squash plants. Female flowers have what looks like a small fruit (ovary) at the base of the flower, while males have nothing. Male flowers will not produce any fruit.

MALE   FEMALE

2. Pick a male flower, and pull off all the petals, exposing the inner stamen and anther, which are covered in pollen. You have now created a pollen "brush."

3. Apply pollen to the stigma (or center) of a female flower with the "brush." After pollination, fertilization occurs and the fruit will develop.

shifts to full-size fruit by midseason, which I consider mature when they are anywhere from 3 to 9 inches long, depending on the squash variety and my plans for them in the kitchen.

I use a sharp kitchen knife to cut the fruits from the plant. When I'm cutting many fruits, I wear latex gloves because the small spines on the leaves can be irritating. You can get latex gloves from your dentist, I assure you.

SECRETS TO
SUMMER SQUASH

A few simple strategies will keep your summer squash going strong all season long. Follow farmers Jo Meller and Jim Sluyter's succession planting plan and care guidelines and the only thing left to do is enjoy your harvest.

THERE IS NO DOUBT ABOUT IT—SUMMER SQUASH IS A PROLIFIC producer. Around here, folks lock their car doors in midsummer, not to prevent theft but to keep gardeners from throwing their excess zucchini into the backseat. We avoid tiring of zucchini by growing a wide range of the tastiest summer squash varieties and harvesting them at their peak. By planting several succession crops, watering the root zone with the help of sunken pots, and smothering weeds with a cover crop, we reap a steady harvest from healthy plants over a long season. This keeps summer squash high on the list of favorites for the members of our community-supported agriculture (CSA) farm.

The family is large and diverse. Although this pattypan squash may look like a gourd, it is not. Like most squashes, this variety is worth growing for its sweet, delectable flavor.

BEGIN SUCCESSION PLANTING WHEN THE SOIL WARMS

We plant half our summer squash when the ground has thoroughly warmed up after the last frost. The soil temperature must be 65°F or higher for good germination. We used to start squash, which has very delicate roots, inside and transplant out after the threat of frost had passed, but we found that seeds planted along with the transplants matured at about the same time. If you need to plant inside because of cool soil, give each plant its own pot and carefully transplant into the garden two weeks later. Squash plants are tender and need protection if a late frost threatens.

A month after the first planting, we do a second sowing. If we can find the space, we will do an additional planting a few weeks after that. We pull out and compost the first plants as they slow down. This gives us young, strong, prolific plants until the first fall frost.

SINK IN POTS FOR CONSISTENT WATERING

When we plant squash in late spring, we are already thinking ahead about how to make summer watering easy. We begin by sowing squash seeds in hills 4 feet apart. To prepare the bed, we mark where the hills will be and dig a hole 2 feet deep by 1 or 2 feet wide. Summer squash requires fertile soil to support its large leaves and rapid growth, so we put in a couple shovelfuls of compost and build a hill with the garden dirt dug from the hole. As we backfill the hole, we bury a 1-gallon nursery pot in the middle (see the sidebar on the facing page). The rim of the pot should be 1 or 2 inches out of the ground when the hill is finished, and there should be no soil in the pot. We plant four to six seeds per hill, about ½ inch deep. We poke them into the ground 2 to 3 inches away from the pots.

Once the seeds have germinated, we thin each hill to the two or three strongest plants. As the plants grow larger, the sunken nursery pots give us the advantage of watering at root level. We also shovel some compost into the pots later in the season to give the plants compost tea as we water. Summer squash is a thirsty plant; we water in the nursery pots once or twice a week, even if there has been rain.

FERTILIZE AND CONTROL WEEDS WITH HAIRY VETCH

When the seedlings are up and thinned, it's time to plant hairy vetch between the hills. The vetch prevents erosion and keeps the ground cooler on hot summer days. It also crowds out most weeds in the space between the hills. But its greatest virtue is that it changes the nitrogen in the air into a form that can be taken up by the squash plants, a process known as nitrogen fixation.

The squash plants are planted around the empty pot, not in it. Three plants per hill is the perfect amount.

A planting of hairy vetch around the hills discourages weeds and feeds the soil.

Filling the empty pot with water allows you to concentrate and evenly disperse moisture.

PLANT A SQUASH HILL

1. PREPARE THE PERFECT HILL.
Dig a hole 2 feet deep, and fill
it half full with compost. This will
encourage vigorous root growth.

**2. ADD A PLASTIC NURSERY
POT.** Place a pot in the center of
the hole, with the lip extending
above the ground by 1 to
2 inches, and backfill the hole.

3. FINISH OFF THE BED. Rake the
soil smooth around the pot, and
gently tamp it down with a soil
rake. Try to avoid getting any soil
in the pot.

To plant the vetch, we cast the seeds thickly on
bare ground, starting about 6 inches from the squash
seedlings, then rake them in and tamp lightly with the
back of the rake. We water frequently until the vetch is
well established. During fall cleanup, we turn it into the
soil to enhance the bed for next year's crop.

It may have a
funny name, but
it's a squash's best
friend. A handful
of hairy vetch
seeds is all that's
needed to keep
the weeds at bay
and give your
plants a nutritious
boost.

WATCH OUT FOR SQUASH BUGS

As the season progresses, one of the first concerns you
may have is that the plants don't appear to be setting fruit.
Squash is not self-pollinating, so bees are important in the
fruiting process. Also, don't worry if some of the flowers
don't set fruit at all. Squash has male and female flowers,
and the males usually bloom first and do not produce fruit.

There are several insects that harm summer squash
crops. One of the most serious is the squash bug, a dingy
brownish insect, which smells awful when crushed. It
resists most organic pesticides, so we handpick the bugs
every couple of days to keep them in check. We look for
their eggs (see the top left photo on p. 134), which are a
little smaller than sesame seeds, shiny and orange-brown,
usually clustered on the underside of the leaves. We scrape
them off carefully but don't worry if we damage the leaf

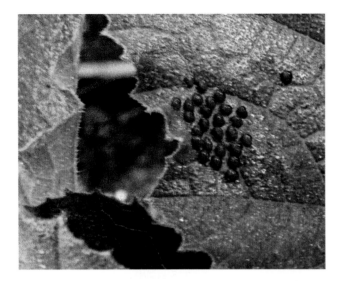

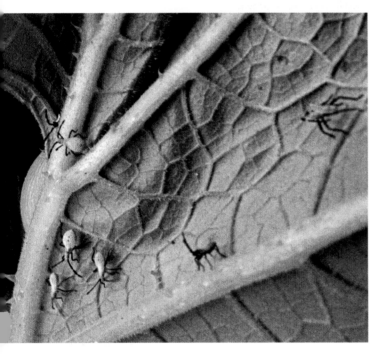

LEFT Learn to identify the bad bugs. Squash bug eggs (top left) are a shiny orange-brown and can be scraped off the leaves with your fingers. In the nymphal stage (bottom left), squash bugs look like big gray aphids.

ABOVE Control infestations as soon as possible. The adult squash bug is an unattractive brown color and has an unappealing smell when crushed. Dropping the bugs into a jar of soapy water is one way to get rid of them.

a little in the process; the insect can do far more harm. We also handpick the nymphs, which look a little like overgrown gray aphids (see the bottom left photo above).

Cucumber beetles in the squash patch can spread bacterial wilt. They prefer cucumbers, but we handpick (you have to be fast!) the few we find on squash. If the vines suddenly wilt, it could be a symptom of bacterial wilt. Remove the infected parts of the plant, but be sure to disinfect your pruners before using them again. There is no treatment for bacterial wilt, so it is important to check frequently for cucumber beetles.

Squash vine borer can also cause wilting leaves. If you suspect vine borer, look for a small hole near the base of

the plant. We usually slit the vine from that point, destroy the borer, and try to save the plant. Be on the lookout for the adult vine borer, a rather pretty, clear-winged moth with a red abdomen—a sure sign of borer activity.

As squash plants age, the leaves often start to turn whitish, most likely from powdery mildew. The plants will still produce fruit for a while after this process begins, but this is the time when we are happy to have planted another crop of squash. Despite these pest and disease problems, succession plantings keep us far enough ahead of the game that we are supplied with summer squash until we have had our fill.

PICK THE RIGHT VARIETIES FOR THE BEST TASTE

Zucchini the size of baseball bats are impressive enough, but they've grown far beyond their best flavor. Since squash can grow rapidly, check plants daily when they start to produce. Keeping the squash picked promotes a steady supply. Summer squash that is too large becomes bland but is still suitable for zucchini bread. For the best flavor, get summer squashes off the vine before they are more than 7 to 8 inches long.

We've tried many varieties, and our longtime favorite is 'Sunburst'. A yellow pattypan or scallopini type of summer squash, it is both attractive and tasty. A Lebanese variety named 'White Bush' (also called Mideast or cousa type) is a bulbous, light green squash with white speckles.

The green zucchini group has many winners, including 'Raven'—our favorite—but 'Black Zucchini' is another nice option. 'Eight Ball' (and its new cousins, 'One Ball' and 'Cue Ball') are interesting for

Zucchini is just the beginning (clockwise from top): 'Eight Ball', 'White Bush', 'Gentry', 'Raven', and 'Sunburst'.

their shape: perfectly round and best when picked at about the size of a billiard ball.

Yellow crookneck and straightneck varieties abound, but our favorites are 'Gentry' and 'Early Prolific Straightneck', respectively.

Growing perfect summer squash is a snap. With consistent water, a bit of fertilizer, and some minor pest control, you can harvest picture-perfect squash like this for months.

WINTER SQUASH
FOR EVERYONE

Don't tell anyone, but this veggie is tastier and easier to grow than you might think. After months of caring for the sprawling vines, your reward is an abundance of these sweet, creamy fruit. Gardening author Amy Goldman shares all her secrets so you can enjoy this fabulous end-of-season treat straight from your garden.

THERE'S NOTHING MORE AMERICAN THAN APPLE PIE. OR IS THERE? Winter squashes belong to the fall season—and to us—in a way that apples (a transplant from Eurasia) never will. Native Americans domesticated squashes from indigenous varieties hundreds of years ago, so this vegetable is built to thrive here. Besides that, who can imagine Thanksgiving without pumpkin pie?

There's more to the world of winter squash, though, than farm-stand pumpkins. Hundreds of varieties exist, but you'll rarely see most of them at your local grocery store. They include everything from garden behemoths, like 'Gill's Blue Hubbard', to the bump-rinded 'Marina di Chioggia'. Best of all, winter squashes are incredibly flavorful, the best ones tasting like chestnuts or sweet potatoes. Growing winter squash is a joy and is fairly easy if a couple of basic rules are followed.

FAR LEFT 'Musquée de Provence' TOP LEFT 'Sugar Loaf' BOTTOM LEFT 'Tennessee Sweet Potato'

INCREASE YIELDS WITH PROPER SPACING

I can't guarantee you a bumper crop, but if you give your winter squash the right conditions and care, your success rate will skyrocket. One of the biggest mistakes gardeners make is to direct-sow or transplant seedlings before the soil has warmed to at least 70°F. Squashes do not tolerate cold temperatures. In short-season areas, start seeds inside three weeks before the frost-free date in spring—but no earlier because older transplants will produce poorly. A garden situated in full sun with warm, well-drained, fertile soil that's slightly acidic (a pH of 6.0 to 6.8) is the ideal spot for squashes. Using compost and soil amendments usually eliminates the need for synthetic fertilizers, which are high in nitrogen or phosphorus and can actually lower fruit quality and yield.

You'll need to space plants far enough apart in the row to give them ample room to flourish. When plants are crowded, fruit yield, size, and quality are reduced (and fungal diseases, like powdery mildew, can fester). Most winter squashes are excessively vigorous growers, with vines that spread out for many feet (unless trellised up); the larger-fruited varieties, like big pumpkins, take up even more space. To reduce competition between plants, I like to space most plants 10 to 12 feet apart.

The lengths of squash branches, however, can vary. So if you don't have a lot of space, try a variety that has shorter vines. Semibush types have shorter internodes (the stem space between each leaf) and branches. These types may also set fruit on vines later in the season. I find

SQUASH BASICS

- Amend beds with compost and manure.
- Plant in rows, spacing hilled plants 6 to 10 feet apart, depending on the variety.
- Use row covers and foil (around the stems) for pest protection.
- Harvest when the rinds harden and change color.

HOW TO CHOOSE THE BEST VARIETY

Winter squashes belong to the genus *Cucurbita*, and because this diverse group originated in the New World, gardeners in North America have a distinct advantage in growing them successfully. Winter squashes fall into four domesticated species groups: *C. maxima*, *C. moschata*, *C. argyrosperma*, and *C. pepo*. Any of these species can be grown by beginning gardeners throughout most of the United States, but where you live dictates which type of winter squash is best for you to grow.

'Buttercup'

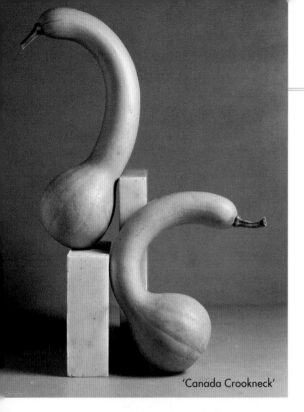

'Canada Crookneck'

WARM AND DRY ALL SEASON LONG

Squashes that belong to the group *C. argyrosperma*, including the cultivars 'Tennessee Sweet Potato' (see the bottom photo on p. 137) and 'Green Striped Cushaw' (below), are the best bet for these conditions.

'Green Striped Cushaw'

'Sibley'

DAMP AND TROPICAL

Try any squash that belongs to the *C. moschata* group, including the delicious and reliable 'Canada Crookneck' (top)and 'Musquée de Provence' (see the photo on p. 136).

A CHILLY SPRING WITH A SHORT GROWING SEASON

The group *C. maxima* tolerates cool temperatures. Some of my favorites are 'Buttercup' (left) and 'Sibley' (above).

'Winter Luxury Pie'

THE HOTTEST OF THE HOT

Gardeners in scorching climates should stick to growing *C. pepo*, the most popular and diverse of the squash species; this group includes pumpkins. Among the most delicious are 'Winter Luxury Pie' (left) and 'Sugar Loaf' (see the top photo on p. 137).

ABOVE LEFT AND RIGHT Hill and cover for the ultimate winter squash harvest. Planting seedlings atop a mound of soil (left) improves drainage, while using floating row covers (above) will help keep the warmth in and the bugs out.

about 8 feet of space between these varieties is adequate. Bush varieties—compact plants with the shortest internodes—don't spread much, which allows closer row spacing of about 6 feet. These varieties also lack tendrils for climbing, so they can't be trellised. 'Gold Nugget' is an excellent squash that grows on short-running vines.

PLASTIC MULCH AND INSECT PROTECTION ENHANCE THE HARVEST

Squashes can be planted in hills or drills. Hills are mounds of soil into which groupings of plants are elevated above the garden surface to improve soil drainage (see the top left photo). Drills are trenches where plants are placed, one at a time down the row, spaced evenly. I use the hill method, allowing two plants per hill for added insurance just in case one of the seedlings dies off. If they are both still thriving after a couple of weeks, I pull out one of the two, leaving behind the strongest seedling.

Black plastic mulch always carpets my winter squash patch. I also cover newly planted seedlings with floating

ABOVE Take pest protection to the next level. Wrap the stems of your seedlings in aluminum foil to prevent the larvae of squash vine borers from burrowing into your plants.

row covers for a few weeks (see the right photo on the facing page). These methods ramp up the heat, protect against soil-borne diseases and insect predators, and produce earlier and more abundant harvests. Plastic mulch also conserves soil moisture and reduces the watering requirements—in midseason, squashes may require up to 2 inches of water weekly. As the plants grow, prune off any defective fruit, but don't prune the vines because that will diminish yield and quality.

Be vigilant about bugs, beetles, and borers as well as fungal and bacterial diseases, because these pests and diseases are known to wreak havoc on a squash patch. You could use an arsenal of toxic chemicals, but I recommend more benign and preventive measures, such as crop rotation and good garden sanitation. These will hit the vine borer, squash bug, and cucumber beetle right where they live (overwintering in spent vines and debris). If these bugs don't have a place to hide out, then maybe they will never take up residence in your garden.

In addition, mechanical barriers, such as row covers, protect young plants against pests and diseases at the start of the plants' life—a time when they are the most susceptible. I also like to wrap a strip of aluminum foil around the stem of the squash plants at soil level (and generally up the stem a few inches) to ward off the larvae of squash vine borers (see the bottom left photo on the facing page). This prevents the maggot-looking worms from tunneling into the stems and causing serious injury, which can result in the plants' demise. Give your squashes another layer of protection by coating the plants—and the ground around them—with powders or dusts, such as diatomaceous earth (an organic pest control made out of crushed sea fossils), or the endotoxin spray *Bacillus thuringiensis* (Bt). Be sure to reapply these substances after it rains. Despite all your preventive measures, you may still notice your vines wilting despite getting adequate water. This means your vines have been infiltrated by a borer. If you're not too squeamish, you can slit the stem of your infected squash vine, remove and eliminate the offender, and let the vine heal itself.

Winter squashes need as much as three to five months of frost-free conditions after sowing to reach maturity. They're ready to harvest when the fruits have reached their maximum size and weight (check the seed-packet specifications) and their rinds have hardened and changed color. With a little effort, you'll be able to pull in a big enough harvest to supply the Thanksgiving table.

HOW TO PRESERVE THE HARVEST

A winter squash is ready to harvest when it resists being punctured by a thumbnail. Cut the fruit from the vine, and move it to a well-ventilated place out of direct sunlight (see the photo below). Clean the squash in a 10 percent chlorine bleach solution to reduce the chances of mold ruining the fruit. Handle with care, and avoid damaging the stem because, if it breaks off, disease can move in and cause spoilage. After curing for two to three weeks, store your winter squash at 50°F to 60°F with a relative humidity of 50 to 70 percent (dry basements work well) until you are ready to use it.

PUMPKINS

Is there anyone out there who doesn't like pumpkin pie? Just mention the word "pumpkin" and most people immediately start drooling, thinking about a slice. To grow your own pumpkins, simply follow these easy steps from market gardener William Brown.

FOR ME, PUMPKINS ARE ONE OF THOSE FOODS THAT BRING UP A host of pleasant memories. As a boy, I remember the rich, spicy aroma of pumpkin pies baking in Grandma's kitchen—a special treat we ate only for Thanksgiving and Christmas. Now that I have more say in the matter of what my family eats, we consume lots of pumpkin: as a vegetable side dish, in breads, in pies and puddings, and even in ice cream.

The pumpkin possesses many desirable characteristics. It is easy to grow, prolific, nutritious, and relatively free from pests and diseases. It stores well and produces edible seeds and meat that can be eaten as either a sweet or savory dish. But the most common use for pumpkins is undoubtedly decorative.

Pumpkins are closely related to squash and grow well in most climate zones, although gardeners in northern areas or at high altitudes will want to use a row cover or some other type of frost protection for cool spring evenings.

Pumpkin plants are either indeterminate creeping vines or determinate shorter vines but not true bushes. They produce both

This family is large and diverse. They can be long and green, flat and red, or perfectly round and orange, but all pumpkins are vegetable garden essentials.

A $25 HOLE FOR A $5 PLANT

To grow the best pumpkins possible, you need to amend your soil before planting. Pumpkins like rich, loamy soil that is well drained but remains moist. Adding things like compost and fertilizer to the planting hole will ensure that your pumpkins grow to their potential.

1. Start by chopping out a hole considerably bigger than the pumpkin seedling. Sometimes the claw end of a steel hammer works best.

2. Add compost and an organic fertilizer mix (recipe, facing page) to your planting hole.

3.. Transplant seedlings when they are eight to 12 weeks old. After planting, make a moat around the transplant so that the water stays where you want it—near the plant.

male and female flowers. The female flowers are open for only one day and will produce pumpkins if pollinated. Sometimes the first female flowers will open before there are any male flowers to pollinate them. They'll dry up and drop off, but the plant will continue to produce flowers.

THE RIGHT VARIETY DEPENDS ON ROOM AND REGION

Besides being easy to grow, pumpkins are available in numerous varieties, each possessing its own appeal. To decide which to plant, consider what you want to do with the pumpkins: eat them as a sweet or savory dish or use them as an autumnal ornament. Also consider whether you are growing pumpkins to store for midwinter dining and how much space you have in the garden.

Whatever you decide, keep in mind the length of your growing season. Most varieties need at least 95 days to mature, with some larger varieties taking as many as 120 days. I have grown pumpkins in areas ranging from Zones 1 to 5, but gardeners as far south as Zone 9 grow them, as well. In the South, pumpkins are generally grown as a winter food crop (they mature at the wrong time of the year for Halloween activities), and they do well even in high heat as long as they have enough water.

I usually grow at least two varieties of small to medium-size pumpkins, and I make sure that at least one variety matures early. My favorites for smaller pumpkins—in the 4- to 10-pound range—are 'New England Pie', 'Rocket', 'Racer', 'Small Sugar', 'Howden', 'Montana Jack', and 'Long Pie', an heirloom that is harvested green and turns orange in storage. While I don't normally grow tiny decorative pumpkins, I have friends who have had great success with 'Jack Be Little' and 'Fairy Tale.'

Pumpkins prefer a well-drained, fertile, loamy soil with a neutral pH, but they will grow in heavier clay soils as long as they are not continually wet. To enrich the soil prior to planting, prepare what my dad used to call a "$25 hole for a $5 plant" (see the sidebar on the facing page). Dig a hole approximately 1 foot deep and 2 to 3 feet wide, then fill it with a mixture of compost, topsoil from the hole, and a blend of organic fertilizers and soil amendments. Then mound the excess soil and compost mixture into a traditional hill.

MOUNDS AND MULCH HASTEN THE HARVEST

Pumpkins like hot feet. The traditional small hill or mound (12 to 18 inches high) will warm up quickly in spring, speeding up seed germination when seeds are sown directly in the ground. The increased warmth of the soil also encourages vigorous root growth. While this is still a sound practice, there is another option: using plastic mulch with or without a row cover. Both hills and plastic mulch increase the soil temperature in the root zone. The floating row cover provides warmth and uniform growing conditions as well as protection from most flying insect pests.

Combining black plastic mulch with row covers gives you a good jump on the season. Lay drip irrigation under the plastic because pumpkins like to be deeply watered. The plastic eliminates the need to weed. When the danger of frost is gone, however, you should remove the row cover to allow the bees to pollinate your crop.

Soil blocks are another option for jump-starting the pumpkin season. If I start the seeds indoors using soil blocks, I can hold off on transplanting my pumpkins until late spring without plants becoming root-bound (see the left photo on p. 146). I put out 8- to 12-week-old plants late in spring and cover them with floating row covers or cloches for protection from late-season frost (see the right photo on p. 146).

Lots of room is important because these sun-loving plants will grow to fill the available space—and then some. I usually grow the indeterminate, creeping-vine type. I plant pumpkins into hills 12 feet apart, then train the vines toward the next hill in the row so that they fill the space in between. Space bush varieties 8 feet apart in all directions. I also spray the plants once or twice during the growing season with a foliar mix of kelp and liquid fish emulsion.

ORGANIC PUMPKIN FERTILIZER

I have been using this formula since 1986, when I had a 5-acre market garden in upstate Minnesota. I needed a baseline mix that would produce good yields. With the help of a chemistry teacher, I developed a mix that works well in warm soil, with enough biological activity to break the fertilizer into a food plants can use.

RECIPE

I fertilize each plant with a mix of:

- 1 cup bonemeal (for phosphorus)
- ¾ cup greensand
- ½ cup blood meal (for nitrogen)
- ⅓ cup kelp meal
- ¼ cup hardwood ashes (for potassium)
- 2 tablespoons agricultural lime (for calcium)
- 2 tablespoons pelleted sulfur

Wood ashes

Greensand

Lime

Bonemeal

Blood meal

FAR LEFT Accelerate the pumpkin season. Soil blocks give seedlings more room to grow, so you can keep them indoors longer.

NEAR LEFT Cloches offer protection from the cold. They also give plants a moist growing environment.

GROW THEM UP INSTEAD OF OUT

When you have a small amount of space, growing pumpkins is usually out of the question. But that doesn't have to be the case. Pumpkins are vines that you can train to grow vertically. In my urban garden, I use a chain-link fence for support. Throughout the growing season, I train the vines to grow up and through the fence. The tendrils also help, by wrapping around the wire fence and supporting the plant as it grows. The best types of pumpkins to grow vertically are smaller varieties, like 'Jack Be Little', a tiny, flat, 8-ounce pumpkin, or 'New England Pie', a 4- to 5-pound sweet pumpkin perfect for pies.
—PATTI MORENO, MASS. GARDENER

AVOID PESTS TO PRESERVE THE PATCH

Once pumpkins are in the garden and growing, they require little maintenance, just consistent watering and a watchful eye for pests: leaf miners, squash bugs, and squash vine borers. You can use neem extracts to control the first two pests. The best strategy for dealing with vine borers is to time plantings so that the vines are mature enough to withstand the damage.

I still have trouble with the squash vine borer. This critter wreaks havoc by attacking the plant at the base of the stem, within 2 inches of the ground. It literally bores a hole into a stem and deposits one or more eggs inside. The eggs hatch within 7 to 10 days. Once hatched, the borer larva eats the soft inner tissue of the plant stem, effectively stopping the flow of nutrients and moisture from the roots to the leaves. Usually, the first thing gardeners notice is that the plant is wilted beyond hope.

Once the larva matures, it crawls out of the stem, burrows into the ground, and metamorphoses into a pupa. The pupa matures and emerges as a flying adult, seeks out a mate, and begins the cycle again. Depending on what zone you live in, there may be two cycles, but most gardeners in northern areas will face only one.

The initial infestation is revealed by a tiny pile of what looks like sawdust at the base of the plant. Keep an eye on your plants, and if you notice this damage, you can surgically remove the larvae by slicing the stem lengthwise and plucking the little beasties out with tweezers. Wrap the stem with breathable adhesive tape, and the plant should heal and continue to grow.

As I mentioned earlier, floating row covers will protect pumpkins (unless larvae hatch out under the row cover), but you will have to pay close attention to pollination. My homemade alternative to borers is to glue a strip of

aluminum foil around the stem before I transplant the seedlings. My "glue" is a mixture of pressed garlic, cayenne, and boiled molasses. I use a wooden spatula to paste the goop on (from the ground up about 6 inches), then wrap foil around it. I secure the shield with a loose twist tie. If you consistently have problems with vine borers, then applying nematodes in the spring is a good idea.

Once you've seen to the basics and have taken care to keep pests under control, all that's left to do is to harvest. You must be patient and wait until fall, after the vines have been killed by frost and the stems are dry and shrunken (see the photo at right). Pumpkins picked before they are mature will be "green" and won't store well. Likewise, be careful not to break the stem off the pumpkin, because that, too, will affect the length of time you'll be able to store it.

After I harvest my pumpkins, I wash them with mild soapy water and rinse them with a mild bleach solution: 1 cup chlorine bleach to 5 gallons cool water. The final rinse helps inhibit mold and other fungal growth while the pumpkins are being stored for later use. When you get ready to use a pumpkin, be careful when cutting it open— and don't forget to clean and toast the seeds. They, too, are scrumptious.

Give them space to ramble. A single pumpkin vine can spread up to 30 feet, so be sure to provide plants with plenty of room to grow (top). You need to wait until all the vines have died before picking pumpkins from your patch (above).

GREENS

CUT-AND-COME-AGAIN
LETTUCE

With a vast array of types, colors, and shapes to choose from, market gardener Peter Garnham reveals his tried-and-true, favorite varieties—and his secrets to year-round growing.

IN MY SMALL MARKET GARDEN, I GROW 100-FOOT-LONG ROWS of lettuce. The rows of green and red varieties, all with different leaf textures, are so pretty it almost seems a shame to harvest the tasty little leaves that local chefs demand for their mesclun mix. But twice a week, I kneel in the white clover pathways to shear the baby plants.

Most of the dozen or so lettuce varieties are the type described as "cutting lettuces," which obligingly and vigorously sprout a fresh crop of leaves when they are snipped off just a couple of inches above the ground. They are often called "cut-and-come-again lettuces."

Cutting lettuces are mostly nonheading leaf varieties from two groups: Grand Rapids and oakleaf. The Grand Rapids group produces broad, crinkled, and frilly leaves, while the oakleaf varieties have flatter and distinctively lobed leaves. Both groups include red and green varieties and several red-green combinations. All make great garden design elements.

Cutting lettuces keep your harvest going—and look beautiful in your garden.

'Black Seeded Simpson'   'Craquerelle du Midi'   'Oakleaf'   'Red Oakleaf'   'Salad Bowl'

PAINT THE GARDEN WITH LETTUCES

Whatever else I grow, I always have plenty of 'Black Seeded Simpson', an heirloom. I don't bother with little packets; I buy it by the ounce, about 25,000 seeds. Properly stored, lettuce seed stays viable for three years.

'Black Seeded Simpson' is so reliable that I use it as the standard for judging the germination success of other varieties. A fast grower, it produces yellowish green leaves. Its only shortcoming is a tendency to bolt in summer heat; it does best in spring and fall here on Long Island.

One of the best summer performers I have found is a romaine: a French cos, 'Craquerelle du Midi'. When every other lettuce in my garden is getting bitter or announcing its plans to set seed, this one stays mild and leafy.

The red- or green-lobed leaves of the oakleaf types are pillars of the loose-leaf establishment. There are at least half a dozen varieties of each color commonly found in seed catalogs. 'Oakleaf' and 'Red Oakleaf' are the original standbys that yield crisp, tender leaves and keep going through moderate heat. Although it has deeply lobed leaves, 'Salad Bowl' is not a true oakleaf. But it is an All-America Selections winner that produces rosettes of delicate, lime green leaves and also has good heat tolerance.

Tops for reliability, even through a hot summer, is 'Red Sails'. Another All-America Selections winner, it's a fast grower with green and reddish bronze leaves.

'Lollo Rossa' has light green leaves with elegant rosy margins, while its cousin, 'Lollo Biondo', is pure pale green. Both 'Lollo' cultivars are deeply curled and heat tolerant, and are decorative in the garden and in salads.

Of the butterheads, 'Ermosa' has dark green leaves and stands up to a fair amount of summer heat. In a weak pre-spring moment, I ordered seed for a romaine called 'Freckles' (also known as 'Trout Back') simply because I liked its name. It is a beautiful lettuce—lime green flecked with wine red markings—and has a fresh, delicate taste.

FOR A BETTER HARVEST, AVOID THINNING

Because they are harvested while very young, cutting lettuces can be planted in fairly dense bands. Instead of casting seed, it is just as easy to sow rows about 3 inches apart, with ½ to 1 inch between plants in the row. I have found that it takes less time to plant seed carefully than to thin seedlings; besides, if not done properly, thinning often disturbs the roots of the seedlings that are left.

There are several ways to sow seed to eliminate thinning. The simplest approach is to mix the seed with dry builder's sand (not salty beach sand), using about twice as much sand as seed. This makes it easier to dribble seeds at fairly even spacing down a marked row. An inexpensive little gadget that distributes seed much better than a seed packet is a seed sower, which has five different-size outlets to control the flow of seeds down a tapered spout.

If enough space is available or you just want to confuse pests, you could sometimes skip the cut-and-come-again routine in favor of a harvest-hoe-rake-and-reseed approach. Harvest the young plants, roots and all; stir up the soil with a stirrup hoe; rake the bed flat; and sow fresh seed.

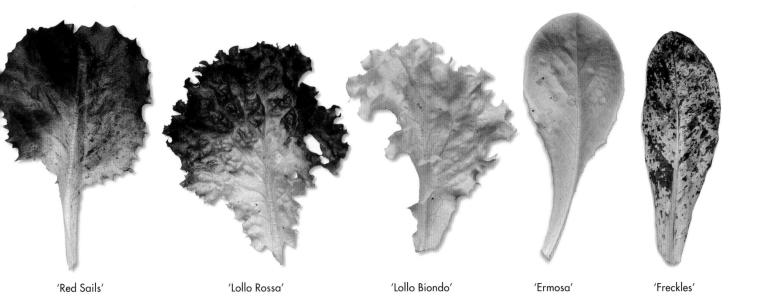

'Red Sails'   'Lollo Rossa'   'Lollo Biondo'   'Ermosa'   'Freckles'

KEEP LETTUCE COMING

Lettuces like a fairly rich, sandy loam. I till the beds and let them settle for a week before applying about an inch of manure or compost, which I work into the near-surface zone with a stirrup hoe. After harvesting leaves, I revive the plants with a weak fish or seaweed emulsion or with manure tea.

Lettuce will grow, if not thrive, in less-than-ideal soil, but one thing it must have is water, about an inch per week. Drip irrigation puts water only where a plant needs it. Overhead watering wastes a lot of water and is usually done at the wrong time, such as late in the day or in hot, muggy weather, which encourages fungal diseases.

GROW IT ALL YEAR LONG

In the home garden, sowing every week will ensure a constant and generous supply of lettuce. Each sowing yields three or four cuttings before the plants are exhausted. As a rough guide to quantity, sowing about a 3-foot-long row every week will keep one omnivorous adult well supplied with salad from spring to fall; a vegetarian might consume twice as much.

Lettuces prefer cool temperatures, but by sowing every week, choosing heat-tolerant varieties, and using shade-cloth tunnels, I can produce lettuce right through my Zone 7 summers. It is easy to keep the supply going right into winter by growing winter varieties in cold frames or tunnels of row-covered fabric. The same tunnels can be used, covered instead with 50 percent shade cloth, to protect heat-sensitive lettuces from the summer sun.

And just because it's hot doesn't mean I stop sowing lettuce. When temperatures hit above 80°F, lettuce seed will not germinate, so I start seeds in flats in a cool room indoors and set the plants in the garden when they have two sets of true leaves.

❀ BUG WATCH ❀

Slugs love lettuce, but luckily they seem to prefer beer. A few saucers of stale beer help them drown their sorrows and themselves. Sugar water also works, but unfortunately, bees like it even more than slugs.

Cutworms can be a hassle, but they usually won't do too much damage to a fairly dense band of plants. Untilled soil can harbor cutworms, so till your beds in spring while the weather is still cold enough to kill overwintered cutworm pupae and eggs. If cutworms become a real problem, add parasitic nematodes to the soil about a week before planting.

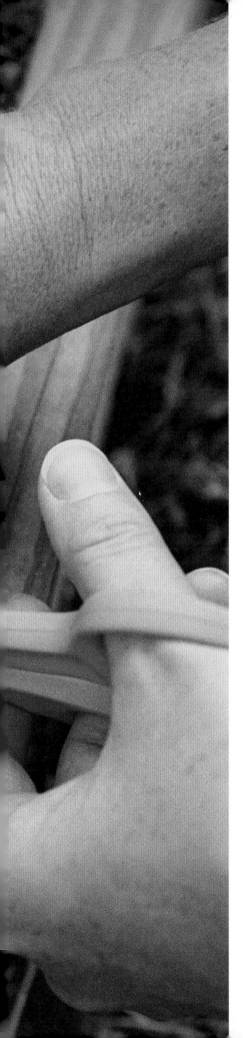

GROW YOUR OWN
MESCLUN MIX

Forget about heads of iceberg—these greens offer more flavor and last longer than any lettuce. The key to tender, succulent mesclun mix, says gardening author Mimi Luebbermann, is to grow it quickly and concentrate on soil preparation.

IN FRANCE, WHERE LETTUCES AND FRESH GREENS REIGN SUPREME, chefs and home cooks fuss over salads as the crowning glory to their meals. A favorite salad is mesclun, a mix of young lettuces, savory herbs, and tender greens. Mesclun was originally a mélange of gathered wild greens and thinnings from the lettuce bed, but now American seed companies offer mesclun mixes—a complete salad from a single packet of seeds. If you have never grown a mesclun mix, you have a great salad adventure ahead of you.

You'll find five to nine types of seeds in each packet of mesclun. Most prepared mixes have been selected so that all the greens in the packet mature at roughly the same time. On occasion, one or two seed varieties will dominate. A well-formulated mix offers convenience and economy—you don't have to buy numerous varieties and grow them separately. A good mix also offers efficiency—a small patch of garden space will yield an entire salad. And if you harvest by the cut-and-come-again method, the same patch will produce three or four cuttings.

Get variety in the bed and the bowl. Mesclun is a mix of greens with many colors, shapes, and flavors. Scissors are the key to harvesting if you want the greens to replenish themselves.

ABOVE Plant in succession for a continuous harvest. Sowing 2-foot-square blocks of mesclun a week or more apart ensures abundance and variety throughout the season.

BELOW It's salad in a seed packet. A mesclun mix might include arugula, mizuna, mustard, cress, or a variety of lettuces.

Mild-flavored mixes combine familiar types of leaf lettuce with savory greens, such as mizuna, red orach, purslane, chervil, and mâche. For a salad with a peppery bite, try a mix containing seeds of cress, Asian mustard, red kale, arugula, red and green chicories, and endive. I prefer spicy mixes over mild ones because the greens in spicy mixes can grow large leaves and still taste good in a stir-fry. In addition, even a little spicy mesclun will spruce up a regular lettuce salad.

Spicy mixes usually include greens that like cool weather, so I start them first in spring and last in fall. In summer, when it's hotter, plant a mild-flavored mix between rows of beans or in an area with morning sun and afternoon shade. I keep patches of both types growing year-round, so I always have variety in my nightly salad bowl.

Mesclun greens will grow back. The sprouts will need thorough watering and fertilizing once a week to ensure multiple harvests.

PLANT MESCLUN FROM SPRING TO FALL

For fresh salads, you'll want to harvest mesclun leaves when they are small and tender, so plant only as much as you can eat regularly. A 2-foot-square block should provide you with enough for several salads over the course of a week. To stretch the harvest, you can mix mesclun with other lettuces. In spring, sow one 2-foot-square block of mesclun each week for a month, and harvest from those blocks until they get tired out.

To be tender and succulent, mesclun needs to grow quickly, so concentrate on soil preparation. Dig your beds carefully, turning in lots of compost to amend the soil and to retain moisture. At the same time, work in some organic, granular fertilizer.

❀ MESCLUN BASICS ❀

- Amend your beds with lots of compost and an organic, granular fertilizer.

- Sow seeds in a 2-foot-square block, covering them with a ¼-inch-deep layer of soil.

- Water well, and mulch to retain moisture.

- Thin plants so that they are roughly 1 inch apart.

- When the greens are 4 to 6 inches long, snip them off just above the crown.

- Water the clipped plants diligently, and fertilize once a week with a diluted solution of fish emulsion.

The ideal size is 4 to 6 inches tall. If the mesclun leaves get any larger, they become stringy and tough.

Because weeds in the bed can cause trouble, I water the well-dug but unplanted bed every couple of days and watch for weeds like a hawk. After two weeks, I hand-weed or lightly hoe, then I plant, knowing that most of the weed seeds have already sprouted.

I sow my blocks thickly but evenly. I sprinkle about ½ teaspoon of seeds in each 2-foot-square block, cover the seeds with soil ¼ inch deep, and pat the soil down firmly. If my attention wanders when sowing, I may overseed an area. In that event, I wait until the lettuce has sprouted and pull some out so that the remaining plants are roughly an inch apart.

I am not, of course, the only one eager for my harvest. Birds, slugs, and snails hover around for a bite as soon as

my back is turned. I take care of the slugs and snails by night-prowling with a flashlight, catching them as they slime toward the young greens. To keep out the birds, I make a miniature row cover with netting and whips from my cottonwood trees.

EVEN MOISTURE LEADS TO A BOUNTIFUL HARVEST

Growing greens closely together shades the soil and preserves moisture for the roots, but I still like to water them overhead just before dark. Although evening watering can encourage mildew and fungus in some plants, the practice has never harmed my mesclun beds.

GIVE YOUR GREENS A BATH

Anyone who has ever grown mesclun knows that it wilts quickly—often as soon as it is plucked from the garden. A few minutes can make the difference between lush leaves and shriveled sticks. To keep the greens fresh, place them directly into a bath of ice water when you harvest them.
—PETER GARNHAM, N.Y. GARDENER

IN EARLY MORNING
Snip off the greens just above ground level, and immediately submerge them in a bowl of icy water. Make sure your bucket has at least a dozen ice cubes floating in it.

BACK IN THE KITCHEN
Pull the leaves out of the bath an spin them dry in a salad spinner. You can also gently blot them dry using paper towels. Store the greens in plastic bags in the refrigerator until you're ready to eat them.

You can water mesclun every day, especially when the weather is hot and dry, but you will save water if you check first to see if watering is really necessary. Because the little plants have shallow roots, it's easy to tell whether the soil is damp or dry simply by sticking a finger into the soil. If the soil is moist and the plants are perky, there's no need to water.

I first tried the cut-and-come-again harvesting technique with half barrels of mesclun that I had planted in my small city garden. I was skeptical as I cut down the young greens with scissors, then amazed to see the leaves begin to grow again soon after being clipped. In the mild climate of the San Francisco Bay Area, where I keep mesclun growing year-round, the cut-and-come-again technique saves me from going to the grocery store for fresh salad greens.

The technique is simple. When the greens are 4 to 6 inches long, snip them off just above the crown, about 1 inch above the soil. Clear-cut an entire salad-size swath at a time. Water the clipped plants diligently, and fertilize once a week with a diluted solution of fish emulsion. Leafy greens will soon reemerge. Depending upon your weather, you may be able to harvest a clear-cut block again within a month. Most blocks yield three or four harvests a season.

LONG-LASTING
SPINACH

Fresh-from-the-garden spinach beats frozen any day. You can get that taste from your own garden if you follow gardener Lucy Apthorp Leske's plan. Just plant the right kinds at the right time so that this crop will go the distance.

THERE WAS A TIME WHEN I HAD TO PICK AND COOK MY ENTIRE spinach crop in two weeks. Depending on how much I'd planted, that could mean eating it daily. The first batch was always a much anticipated, mouthwatering treat, a far cry from the store-bought spinach we'd been eating all winter. By the end of the short harvest season in June, however, I felt like a used-car salesperson when I hawked spinach for dinner.

Things are different now. I can harvest spring spinach from my Nantucket garden over a considerably longer period—from late April to late June—and in quantities my family can easily consume in a meal. I also get a fall crop. This isn't a case of new-and-improved spinach varieties at work. Credit goes to a combination of timed plantings matched with the right varieties or cultivars. In short, I've learned to finesse the spinach harvest.

The spinach season doesn't have to be short. By using succession planting for a few select varieties, you can harvest these sweet leaves for months.

SUCCESSION-PLANTING GUIDE FOR SPINACH

A good way to lengthen the harvest of this tasty green involves a combination of varieties and a nearly year-round approach to planting.

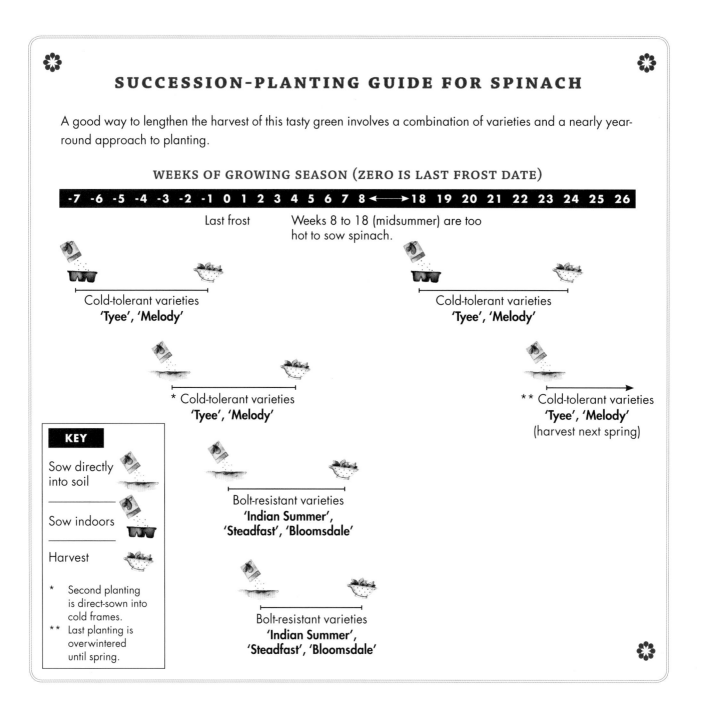

WEEKS OF GROWING SEASON (ZERO IS LAST FROST DATE)

| -7 | -6 | -5 | -4 | -3 | -2 | -1 | 0 | 1 | 2 | 3 | 4 | 5 | 6 | 7 | 8 | ←→ | 18 | 19 | 20 | 21 | 22 | 23 | 24 | 25 | 26 |

Last frost

Weeks 8 to 18 (midsummer) are too hot to sow spinach.

Cold-tolerant varieties
'Tyee', 'Melody'

Cold-tolerant varieties
'Tyee', 'Melody'

* Cold-tolerant varieties
'Tyee', 'Melody'

** Cold-tolerant varieties
'Tyee', 'Melody'
(harvest next spring)

Bolt-resistant varieties
**'Indian Summer',
'Steadfast', 'Bloomsdale'**

Bolt-resistant varieties
**'Indian Summer',
'Steadfast', 'Bloomsdale'**

KEY

Sow directly into soil

Sow indoors

Harvest

* Second planting is direct-sown into cold frames.
** Last planting is overwintered until spring.

CHOOSE VARIETIES BASED ON CLIMATE

Since I started growing vegetables 29 years ago, spinach has been the core of my early spring garden. Spinach needs temperatures of 45°F to 70°F to germinate and to produce thick bunches of sweet, juicy leaves. Any colder and the spinach won't grow; any warmer and it bolts.

It took me a few years to learn how to get spinach growing in the garden sooner and take better advantage of cool weather. The first thing I figured out was how to use different varieties to extend the harvest season. Most spinach matures in about 45 days, unlike, say, corn or tomatoes, which have wide-ranging maturity schedules. Choosing different varieties, therefore, does not, by itself, stagger maturity dates and lengthen the harvest season.

Spinach varieties are distinguished, instead, by their resistance to bolting, downy mildew, or cold. These factors allow me to match varieties with the time of the year they will be actively growing. 'Melody' and 'Tyee', for instance,

tolerate the cold because they germinate in cold soil and resist disease well. 'Indian Summer', 'Steadfast', and 'Bloomsdale' tolerate the heat better and resist bolting for a week or more longer than cold-tolerant varieties. Most spinach varieties taste about the same if grown well.

DEVELOP A PLANTING STRATEGY

In addition to growing different varieties, I've developed a planting plan that covers much of the year. In late February, I start by sowing a few dozen plants' worth of cold-tolerant varieties indoors in six-packs. In late March, I plant the seedlings directly in soil inside a cold frame in the garden. I plant in small batches, having found that about three dozen plants in a 6-foot-long row will provide eight to 10 servings of spinach and several salads.

Also in late March, I direct-sow another 6-foot-long row of the same varieties alongside the transplants in the garden. The cold frame protects the seeds and seedlings from late-winter weather. As soon as soil can be worked, I do two direct sowings: one in mid-April and one in late April. Because these last spring plantings will mature in late June, I choose bolt-resistant varieties. I plant them where they'll receive a little afternoon shade from my shrubs, which helps forestall bolting.

I hold off sowing for several weeks to avoid the hot months of July and August. In mid-August, to prepare for a quick fall crop, I'll start more seed in six-packs for transplanting in the garden. In late September, I scatter the seed of a cold-tolerant variety over a 3-foot-square plot in the garden. Spinach seedlings are extremely hardy, even in my Northeast garden, and some varieties will last over winter with just a bit of help. I sow the seeds where they're most likely to receive late-winter and early spring sun. Once seedlings are up and temperatures drop below freezing at night, I cover the seedlings with straw mulch for winter. In places where snow cover is reliable all winter, mulch isn't necessary. If all goes right, I'll be harvesting again in early spring. This plan ensures that I will have a consistent supply of spinach that does not overwhelm me all at once. The sidebar on p. 162 offers a visual representation of the succession planting plan.

A HEALTHY HARVEST

My spinach produces its first leaves for salads around mid-April, from the overwintered sowing. If the early spring is cold and rainy, I occasionally cover the crop I sowed in fall with a clear plastic tent to speed up the process. I harvest individual outer leaves with a quick twist and pinch when they are about 3 inches long, leaving at least six central leaves remaining on the plant to continue photosynthesizing. I don't harvest whole plants unless I'm thinning the rows.

Spinach plants pass so quickly from adolescence to maturity that a single plant's ability to produce large succulent leaves lasts for only a couple of weeks. Once a plant bolts, I stop picking its leaves and, often, just pull the whole thing out.

My spinach system may seem to demand much planning and organized behavior. But oddly, I do not consider myself an organized gardener. Although I have learned, over the years, that the best gardens require some planning, I've found that habitual puttering drives success. Visiting the garden briefly every day, popping in seeds or plants wherever there's an opening, and growing small batches of backup seedlings indoors year-round yields a spinach crop my family and I can enjoy at our leisure.

CHARD
ALL SEASON LONG

The subtle sweetness of chard isn't its only selling point. Unlike many greens, this crop thrives through the heat of summer and past the first frost. Garden designer Laura McGrath shows you how to get a great harvest.

I DID NOT BEGIN GARDENING OR COOKING FOR LOVE OF CHARD, but once my repertoire expanded beyond tomatoes and basil, chard caught my attention. This green now holds a special place in my garden for its beauty, generous yields, and undemanding ways. The tall sprays of deeply crinkled green leaves and colorful, broad stalks are eye-catching.

Chard makes the late-summer garden look lush, even when the tomatoes are devastated by wilt and the beans are disappearing under hordes of Mexican bean beetles. Unlike many greens, chard will produce steadily through the hottest days of summer and the first autumn frosts. If you pick the outer stalks, new ones will emerge. I use tiny chard leaves in salads, where their sweet flavor comes through. Larger leaves are best when lightly steamed, and they can be substituted for spinach in most recipes. I consider chard stalks a bonus that comes with the tasty greens. When steamed or stir-fried, the stalks have a mild flavor and pleasant crunch.

Harvest the colorful stalks and the green leaves.
With chard, all parts of the plant are edible and
exceptionally flavorful.

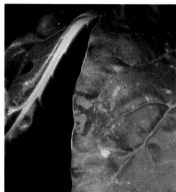

Thin out a robust crop. After the chard seedlings reach about 3 inches tall, pull some out so that each plant is 6 inches from its nearest neighbor.

Pests will leave their mark. Slugs love chard and left unchecked will make small holes in the leaves (at left in photo). Leaf miners, on the other hand, leave scars and lines that look like burns on the foliage (at right in photo).

DIRECT-SOW IN SPRING

Chard is a biennial and a member of the beet family. Although it will overwinter in most gardens, it will set seed during its second year, so it's best to plant a new crop each year. Sow chard seeds ½ inch deep directly into the ground when spring takes a warm turn. In my suburban Boston community garden, that's generally in late April.

Chard that's started in pots and then transplanted is never as vigorous as plants sown directly in place. The difference in size and ultimate yield is remarkable. Every year, though, I ignore my own advice and transplant one or two seedlings, just to fill gaps in a row. It never works—those plants are always noticeably stunted compared with their neighbors.

Chard prefers a slightly alkaline soil, moderately enriched with compost. When seedlings are about 3 inches tall, thin them to stand 6 to 12 inches apart. Use the wider spacing for white-stalked Swiss chard, the largest variety, and slightly tighter spacing for ruby chard or rainbow-chard mixes.

Regular watering of young plants is important. Chard makes few demands as it grows, but the key to vigorous mature plants is regular watering when the plants are small. Never let the young greens struggle in dry soil for more than a day. Once mature, at about a foot tall, the plants are far more tolerant of dry conditions and seem to produce equally well whether pampered or neglected.

This fits my gardening habits well. I fuss over my spring garden in May and June, but by July, I prefer to spend considerably less time in the hot sun—and most of that, harvesting, watering, or staking tomato plants. The chard flourishes whether or not my care is consistent, although a good mulching undoubtedly helps.

Slugs and leaf miners are the only garden pests to bother chard. Row covers will protect against leaf-miner damage by preventing the adult miner from laying eggs on the leaves. The eggs develop into larvae that feed on the chard, leaving distinctive squiggly lines on the leaves. In my garden, leaf-miner damage occurs in July, just as the plants mature, and disappears by August. Slugs rarely make a dent in a mature chard plant before I discover and destroy them.

If you enjoy tender chard seedlings in salads, make successive plantings in spring and early summer, remembering to water consistently. Then harvest the entire plant when young. I prefer to make one spring sowing, enjoy the tender greens in June, and harvest the mature leaves all summer and fall. The cultivar 'Bright Lights', however, works well as a cut-and-come-again green.

CHOOSE THE VARIETY BASED ON FLAVOR

Classic Swiss chard, with its white stems and puckered leaves, is a bit sweeter than red chard. Swiss chard is my first choice for a side dish of steamed greens. Wash the leaves, and shake them dry. Remove the stalks and ribs, and tear the leaves into 3-inch-long pieces. Place them in a wide skillet, cover, and steam until barely wilted. Sprinkle with your favorite vinegar, and serve.

Red-chard leaves are not as heavy as other chards and work well when combined with other ingredients. 'Rainbow Silverbeet' and 'Bright Lights' are small plants, like red chard, but with savoyed (crinkled) leaves that resemble Swiss chard. They are excellent ornamental choices and have a nice flavor.

If you want a supply of summer greens, be sure to grow some Swiss, ruby, or multicolored chard. Once cooked, all chard leaves look pretty much the same. The fun of growing all three is in being able to select a white, red, or pastel stalk as a contrast to other elements in a recipe.

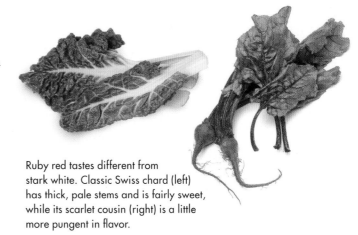

Ruby red tastes different from stark white. Classic Swiss chard (left) has thick, pale stems and is fairly sweet, while its scarlet cousin (right) is a little more pungent in flavor.

 ## USE CHARD TO DRESS UP THE GARDEN

'Bright Lights' (pictured) is the showiest cultivar of chard. It was named a 1998 All-America Selections winner, and it looks great with hot-colored annuals, like marigolds and zinnias. It has lightly savoyed leaves of green and burgundy, and its stems come in red, yellow, pink, gold, and white. I plant a cutting border of annuals and 'Bright Lights' chard in my vegetable garden and a similar border beside my kitchen porch. It's such a striking combination in the garden that you'll hate to harvest it.

GET A HEALTHY BOOST WITH
KALE

These vitamin-packed greens thrive in the garden late in the season when nothing else does. Just select your variety carefully with the help of farmer Nan Wishner.

WHEN I TELL PEOPLE I GROW KALE IN MY VEGETABLE GARDEN, they often give me funny looks and ask why I bother. Even my next-door neighbors, who welcome all my other spare vegetables, refuse my kale—except for an occasional leaf to feed their pet lizard. People think of it as something unpleasant to eat but good for you, like cod liver oil.

But I am here to say that while kale, with its rich dowry of nutrients, is good for you, it is also delicious fresh from the garden. It is easy to grow and beautiful to look at, both in the garden and on your plate. Although a couple of frosts will make it sweeter, gardeners in all climates can grow sweet-tasting kale by choosing the right varieties.

A garden full of kale varieties brings different colors, textures, and flavors.

ABOVE LEFT It looks rough but tastes sweet. Its resemblance to a dinosaur's hide is the reason 'Lacinato' is sometimes called dinosaur kale.

ABOVE RIGHT 'Scotch' kale is almost as beautiful as it is delicious. The fluffy texture of this selection makes it unique—but it does need a nip of frost to become sweet enough to eat.

LEFT Harvest kale from fall through spring. Start by removing the lowest leaves first and then work your way slowly up the main stalk.

PICK A VARIETY BASED ON YOUR REGION

The relationship between kale and weather is simple: Cold temperatures make kale sweet; warm temperatures cause kale to bolt. I used to live in Albany, a small town across the bay from San Francisco, where our winter temperatures seldom went much below 30°F. Our summer mornings and late afternoons were often filled with fog that creeps in over the Golden Gate, leaving a window of mild summer weather in between. Because I had neither extremes of heat nor cold, I needed varieties of kale that would sweeten with a light chill, wouldn't taste too astringent in the absence of severe cold, and wouldn't bolt at the first rise in temperature.

I love 'Scotch' kale (syn. 'Dwarf Blue Curled Scotch') with its curly, thick leaves, the kind most commonly found in produce departments. 'Scotch' kale, unfortunately, needs colder weather than I had to become sweet enough for my taste. That's not a problem, because I love two other kinds of kale even more. 'Red Russian' kale has toothy, blue-green leaves; burgundy trim; and a milder, sweeter bite than 'Scotch' kale. Also known as 'Ragged Jack', 'Red Russian' is an American heirloom that stays

---

KALE BASICS

- Enrich soil with compost or manure.

- Start kale in late winter to early spring, and again in midsummer.

- Sow seeds in cell packs, or scatter in rows 18 inches apart. Cover with ½ inch of soil.

- Place paper-cup collars around the new seedlings to deter slugs and snails.

- Thin seedlings to 12 to 18 inches apart when they are 6 inches tall.

sweet in warm weather. My other favorite is 'Lacinato', an Italian heirloom that produces sweet, midnight green leaves shaped like the long oval end of a lacrosse stick. The young leaves are a lighter green.

In my Albany garden, I would sow kale twice a year, once in midsummer for harvesting in fall through winter, and again in winter for spring harvesting. If you live in a colder climate—like I do now—sow kale in midsummer for a fall harvest. You can also plant kale in early spring and harvest it until the leaves toughen in the heat and the plants go to seed.

AMEND, SOW, THEN THIN FOR THE BEST HARVEST

Every year, I rotate crops and grow a green manure, like red clover, in the beds not producing a winter vegetable. In spring, I dig in the green manure with an inch or two of homemade compost, sometimes supplemented by kelp meal and a little chicken manure. Where the soil is overly acidic, wood ash or other alkaline amendments are good for kale. If my kale ever looks peaked, I feed it a little fish emulsion.

Direct-sown plants work as well as transplants in my garden. I get a crop quicker if I sow the seed directly because the days to harvest stated on the seed package don't seem to include the five or so weeks it takes to grow the seedlings indoors. But I can protect the tiny plants from snails and slugs better if I start them indoors. I thin seedlings so that they're 12 to 18 inches apart; 12 inches is enough for 'Lacinato', but 'Red Russian' needs 18 inches. If they still get too crowded, I harvest the in-between plants and use their leaves for salads or stir-fries. My plants grow anywhere from 18 inches to 3 feet tall.

When I order kale seeds, I look for ones that are not treated with fungicide. Seeds are treated so that they will not decay if planted in cold, wet soil, but I prefer to risk a little seed decay to keep my garden as organic as possible.

The taste and texture of kale harvested and cooked the same day is well worth the few minutes of cabbage-worm patrol each week. Kale that sits in the grocery store gets tough and spicy, while fresh leaves are always crisp, tender, and bittersweet. My kale plants grow tall on increasingly bare stems as I harvest the outer leaves. The lower, outer leaves of 'Red Russian', however, become tough as the season progresses, so I compost them and eat the smaller inside leaves.

When summers are cool, my kale plants may produce for a full year without flowering. Frequently, however, a sunny, warm period sends them all to seed.

CERTAIN PESTS WILL EAT YOUR KALE

In my yard, the most serious threats to kale are cabbage loopers and cabbage worms, green caterpillars hatched from tiny eggs laid on the leaves by cabbage moths. As soon as the weather warms and I see the first brown or white moths flying frenziedly over my greens, I begin carefully inspecting both sides of my kale leaves and removing or crushing the tiny white or orange eggs (see the photo near right).

If I am not vigilant, leaves with holes and scalloped edges are my reward, along with juicy green caterpillars that ride into the kitchen on the harvest (see the photo far right). The caterpillars can be hard to spot because they look like the ribs of the leaves. 'Red Russian' and 'Lacinato' kale are also susceptible to aphids. I crush the clusters of aphids with my fingers or spray them off with the hose.

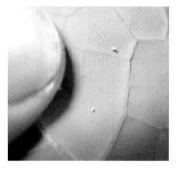
Moth eggs

Caterpillar damage

BOUNTIFUL
BROCCOLI RAAB

Packing a pungent punch, this delicious Italian green is easy to grow and versatile in the kitchen. You can enjoy two crops a year if you follow cookbook author Edward Giobbi's plan.

ON A TRIP THROUGH GERMANY IN 1971, I TOOK A TRAIN FROM Frankfurt to Munich. The train was half empty, and I looked around for a while before finding a friendly face. He was a factory worker in Germany but was originally from Italy. I don't think we had talked more than three minutes before we were on the subject of food. He asked me if I had tasted pasta with *broccoletti di rape*. I assured him that I had, and he clasped his hands, rolled his eyes, and exclaimed in his beautiful dialect, "It's so good it hurts!" What he called *broccoletti di rape*, or *rape* (pronounced *rah-PAY*) for short, is better known in this country as broccoli raab. However you pronounce or spell it, this marvelous cool-weather vegetable is a joy to grow and to cook with.

Broadcast the seed over rough ground. The less-than-ideal soil cradles rainwater for this moisture-loving, cool-weather crop.

> ### BROCCOLI RAAB BASICS
>
> - Amend beds with compost and manure.
> - Plant in late summer and early winter in cool zones or in late fall in warmer spots.
> - Broadcast the seed over the bed, and water the seed in.
> - Harvest as soon as the buds appear (the plants will be between 1 and 2 feet tall).

LEFT Broccoli raab is distinct from broccoli despite its name. It tastes like a combination of turnip greens and broccoli florets.

ABOVE Fall flowers promise a spring crop. Left to flower, broccoli raab will produce seed that overwinters and germinates when the weather warms up.

SOW IN LATE SUMMER AND EARLY WINTER

One of the best things about broccoli raab is how easy it is to grow. Once sown, it requires practically no care at all. Unseasonably warm weather may cause it to bolt too quickly, and deer can be a problem. The only other trouble used to be the unavailability of seeds. Decades ago, I had to get mine from Italy. Today, seeds of broccoli raab are readily available from American seed companies.

Broccoli raab has a penchant for cool, wet weather. Here in the Northeast, I sow two plantings. I sow my first planting in late August or early September and harvest it from late October through November. I sow my second planting after a hard freeze; these seeds hunker down for the winter, then produce an early spring crop. I also allow some of the plants from the first planting to go to seed in late fall so that the seeds will germinate in spring.

I plant a 15-foot-square bed of raab—but then, I'm quite fond of it. A bed 2 feet wide and 12 feet long will yield plenty for the average gardener. Raab likes cool, wet, fertile soil. Last year, I sowed my first planting after a crop of fava beans. I didn't make a fuss about soil preparation. I yanked out the fava beans, broke up the worst clods with a garden fork, and left the soil rough. I find that rough soil does a better job of holding moisture than does finely tilled and smoothly raked soil.

ABOVE Harvest broccoli raab the moment that buds appear. If some plants get away from you, let them seed the next crop.

RIGHT Yes, you can eat it all. From the bottom leaves to the tender tops, every part of this veggie tastes good.

A MISUNDERSTOOD MEMBER OF THE FAMILY

Broccoli raab is sometimes mistaken for turnip greens—and for good reason. One of the Brassicaceae, raab is a cousin of the turnip (*broccoletti* is Italian for "little broccoli," and *rapa* means "turnip"), grown not for its root but for its leaves, shoots, and florets.

Raab is one of the most popular vegetables in Italy, favored for its slight bitterness, which is a little like that of mustard greens with a hint of broccoli, although all comparisons fall short of capturing raab's unique flavor.

HARVEST AT THE FIRST SIGHT OF BUDS

Following the advice of my father and grandfather, I broadcast the seeds thinly and evenly, as I would lettuce, aiming to cover the bed so that the plants are about 3 inches apart. Because it's impossible to space the seeds precisely and because some of them won't germinate, I always sow twice as much seed per given area as is recommended on the package. I don't bother to cover the seeds with soil, but I do water the bed right after sowing so that the water pushes the seeds into the ground. If a dense patch crops up, I thin it and eat the tender stalks and leaves.

I harvest broccoli raab as soon as the buds appear (the plants will be between 1 and 2 feet tall). I check the bed often because the buds burst into flower soon after they form (see the photo at right on the facing page). Using a knife, I cut the main stem several inches below the bud, taking the bud and stem, along with side shoots and leaves—all of which are tender and edible. Broccoli raab produces tender second cuttings, so I leave behind the rest of the main stem because the plant will send up another shoot. This second growth produces smaller, more delicate leaves and buds, called *cime di rape*.

Many Italians favor *cime di rape* over the first cutting, but I prefer the larger buds. In any case, *broccoletti di rape* and *cime di rape* taste best when they've been nipped by a light frost. I can scarcely imagine autumn without them.

HERBS

BASIL BASICS

Bunches of fragrant, delicious basil are within reach—just follow herbalist Susan Belsinger's advice for the most abundant crop. She'll tell you everything you need to know to start from seed successfully.

THE FIRST TIME I TASTED PESTO WAS ON A WARM SUMMER NIGHT while dining alfresco at a restaurant in Fiesole, Italy. My plate of pasta arrived with a bright green aromatic herbal sauce that tasted rich, savory, sweet, and pungent—all at the same time. I couldn't figure out what the main ingredient of the sauce was. With some amusement, my Italian friends explained to me that basil was the key ingredient in this sauce called pesto. That dish changed my life.

Before I left Italy, my friends taught me how to make my own pesto, and the following year, I started growing basil in my garden. I discovered that basil is an easy plant to grow, its only major requirements being full sun and consistent water. Its delicious flavor has made it the most useful herb in my summer kitchen. Although most varieties are grown for their culinary uses, several varieties have compact habits or purple foliage and are useful as ornamental plants, too.

For the best harvest, give plants full sun,
ample water, and regular pruning.

STARTING BASIL IS SIMPLE

- **WHEN DO I START?** Start basil by seed four to six weeks before your last frost date. Plant them outside after all danger of frost has passed and the ground has warmed up.

- **WHAT DO THEY NEED?** Plant basil in good garden soil in full sun. For optimal growth, water, fertilize, and prune plants on a regular basis.

- **HOW DO I GET THE BEST FLAVOR?** For the best-tasting leaves, don't let the plant flower. Prune it every four weeks just above the bottom two sets of leaves.

As seedlings, basils don't like to be overwatered, but in the garden, they don't like to dry out.

For an abundant harvest, fill a 4-foot-wide by 8-foot-long bed with 'Fino Verde' (front), 'Genovese' (middle), and 'Opal' and 'Purple Ruffles' (far corner).

SEEDS PROVIDE THE BEST VARIETY

Most garden centers sell transplants of ornamental and edible basil in spring. But to get the most interesting varieties, I start mine from seed. I start the seeds indoors, four to six weeks before I plan to transplant them into the garden. I fill small flats or seed-starting pans with a soilless medium, sprinkle the surface with seeds, and cover them with plastic wrap. I keep the flats warm but out of direct sun. When the first seed sprouts, I remove the plastic and place the flat either in direct light or 2 to 3 inches below grow lights. Because basil seedlings cannot tolerate overwatering, I don't water them the first day after removing the plastic. I'm careful to allow the growing medium to almost dry out between waterings. As the plants grow, I feed them liquid fertilizer once a week.

When the seedlings have developed their first set of true leaves, usually two to three weeks after germination, I transplant them into small pots. A few weeks later, I begin hardening them off by putting them outside during the day when temperatures are warmest to get them used to outdoor conditions. I eventually leave them outside overnight when I'm sure there won't be any frost.

I transplant my basil plants into the ground in mid- to late May, well after the last frost in my Maryland garden. I plant them in full sun, fertilizing and watering each one well at planting time. I continue to fertilize the plants every two to three weeks, and I water them if we don't get regular rain because basils don't like to dry out.

It is important to keep basils cut back so that you have a continual harvest of fresh leaves throughout the season.

MATCH THE VARIETY TO THE USE

PESTO BASILS

TYPES: 'Genovese', 'Italian Pesto', 'Profuma di Genova'
COMMENTS: The best options for making pesto, these varieties are aromatic, full of flavor, and vigorous growers. They have a lovely scent—a balance of citrus oil, licorice, cinnamon, spice, and mint.

LETTUCE-LEAF BASILS

TYPES: 'Napoletano', 'Lettuce Leaf', 'Mammoth'
COMMENTS: Characterized by huge leaves (5 to 6 inches long and 3 to 4 inches wide), these varieties are perfect for sandwiches and salads. Their flavor includes notes of mint, anise, and citrus.

LEMON BASILS

TYPES: 'Mrs. Burns', 'Sweet Dani'
COMMENTS: Lemon basils are good in vinaigrettes, especially with vegetables and seafood, but they shine in beverages and desserts.

TOP TO BOTTOM
'Italian Pesto'
'Lettuce Leaf'
'Sweet Dani'

Prune regularly for the best flavor. About every four weeks, prune basil back to just above the bottom two sets of leaves. If the plant is allowed to flower, it will lose its flavor.

I am diligent about pruning my plants, and as a result, I get 15 to 25 cups of leaves from each plant per season. It is also important not to let the plants slated for culinary use flower or else the leaves will begin to taste bitter.

Immediately after planting, I prune my basils by cutting them back to just above the bottom two sets of leaves. This early pruning may seem drastic, but it actually stimulates growth. Depending on the weather and how quickly the plants are growing, I prune the plants back again to just above the bottom two sets of leaves about every four weeks—or sooner if they show any signs of flowering.

My passion for basil has continued to grow over the years. Last summer, I grew more than 40 basil plants of assorted varieties, and each one had a delectable fragrance and flavor to offer. Who would have known that a dinner in Italy years ago could have started such a love affair?

ROSEMARY
FOR EVERY GARDEN

No one should be without this flavorful and problem-free herb, says cookbook and gardening author Sylvia Thompson. Follow a few simple steps and this aromatic herb will thrive in your kitchen garden.

AMONG THE FEW HERBS THAT ARE A MUST FOR EVERY KITCHEN garden, rosemary (*Rosmarinus officinalis*, Zones 8–11), most would agree, is preeminent. There's a rosemary to grace nearly every garden and one for almost every purpose. When considering shapes and sizes, you'll find prostrate rosemaries in trailing and creeping forms. These can be used as ground covers or planted so that they spill over a wall or cascade down a bank. Their strong roots make them excellent for erosion control. Prostrate forms are also beautiful hung from a basket or trained as a bonsai.

While prostrate forms grow outward, shrub rosemaries grow upward. Shrubs come in dwarf, medium, and tall sizes, with compact, open, or spiraling habits. Dwarf rosemaries can make a decorative border, while taller shrubs can create an informal screen or even a hedge.

No matter what the palette of flowers in your kitchen garden, there is a rosemary that will complement it. The blossoms are commonly blue, but the blue can be intense or muted. A touch of

Dwarf varieties form perfect edges. Because of their squat, compact habit, small cultivars of rosemary are well behaved and at home in formal gardens, like this English-style one.

blue makes reds, yellows, and oranges sparkle, so some form of blue-flowering rosemary is ideal for a mixed border. Pink-flowering and white-flowering rosemaries can highlight a pastel, silver, or white garden. For intriguing year-round color, variegated rosemary has green needles threaded with gold.

Rosemaries are tender-perennial shrubs and can be early bloomers. In temperate climates, some bloom in December. In our California mountain garden, most have finished flowering before the roses start forming buds. Generally, rosemary blossoms from early spring through early summer and sometimes again in early fall.

GIVE ROSEMARY LIGHT AND LEAN SOIL

All culinary rosemaries originate from Spain, Portugal, and the Mediterranean. Thanks to its heritage, rosemary is rugged. It can handle suffocating heat, stiff winds, salt air, and droughts, and it actually prefers lean, rocky, alkaline soil. Rosemary's gently curving or gnarled branches are stunning and sculptural. Even better, rosemary isn't bothered by deer and other devouring critters.

There are, naturally, elements that will polish off a plant. Too much watering and fertilizer result in woody branches that turn brittle and break. Bad drainage rots

 ABOVE Tall rosemaries can grow into shrubs. If large plants get too woody or out of control, you can prune the plants back after they flower. Never cut away more than half, however.

LEFT It creeps, and it leaps. Prostrate rosemary works well as a ground cover but also looks great when it's allowed to cascade over a wall.

roots. Poor air circulation results in loss of leaves and perhaps even a fatal fungus. A hard freeze kills most plants, but the cultivar 'Arp' can survive at temperatures of 10°F or lower.

It's fairly simple to avoid trouble with rosemary. Just bear in mind its Mediterranean origins. Set it in light, alkaline soil; keep it slightly moist until the plant is established (perhaps a full season); then keep it on the dry side, although the roots should never completely dry out. In the desert, deeply water rosemary several times a year. Should the leaves look dull, the plant needs water. If water doesn't quickly drain from a test hole where you would

TIPS FOR OVERWINTERING ROSEMARY

If you live in an area where rosemary isn't hardy, you can still coax plants through the winter. Here's a foolproof method I like:

SELECT A FEW STOCKY PLANTS TO OVERWINTER

Around midsummer, I lightly prune my plants to encourage short, bushy growth. Then, before nighttime temperatures fall below 50°F, I pot them up, leave them outdoors for a few days to acclimate, and bring them in before the deepening cold induces dormancy.

PLACE THE POTTED PLANTS IN A WARM, SUNNY SPOT

The temperature should be above 50°F and should receive five to six hours of bright, indirect sunlight. If growth is leggy, you can supplement natural light with fluorescent light.

WATER WHEN YOU REMEMBER

Because rosemary is prone to root rot and—equally nasty—powdery mildew, you want to keep roots on the dry side. In the spring, I harden off the plants and set them back into the ground.

like the plant to grow, dig in sand or even pea gravel and turn that spot into a mound or raised bed.

Where growing conditions are ideal, rosemary does not need fertilizing. Where rosemary struggles, feed annually with liquid fish emulsion and kelp solution. Ample breathing space is essential.

Wherever you plant it, set rosemary where you will brush against it. The aroma will catch you by surprise, and, for an instant, you'll be on a Mediterranean shore.

PAY ATTENTION TO THE HARDINESS ZONE

In Zones 6 and below (where winters reach 0°F or colder), grow rosemary in a pot year-round, bringing it indoors before autumn's first killing frost. Some recommend growing it as an annual, but I think that's a waste of a magnificent plant. In Zone 7 (10°F down to 0°F), grow the new plant in a pot the first season, overwinter it indoors, then plant it out in a sheltered spot in spring after hardening it off. In Zones 8 and above (10°F or warmer), you can keep rosemary in the ground.

When there is wet snow, you must support the plant's long branches. During a recent winter, we had more than 3 feet of very wet snow, a first for us. Having had no experience with it, I realized one day that our 5-foot-tall 'Tuscan Blue' rosemary had disappeared. When the snow melted, I found many of the plant's branches broken. Our old 'Arp' is enormous and bushy and on a slope, but it, too, had lost branches, as had new prostrate

MAKE MORE ROSEMARY

As far as herbs go, rosemary is one of the easiest to propagate. The best way to make more plants is with cuttings. Although you can try growing this herb from seed, the germination rate is fairly poor. Follow these simple steps to achieve success with rosemary propagation.
—SUSAN BELSINGER, MD. HERBALIST

 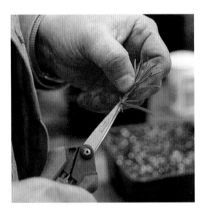 

1. In late fall or early winter, take a 2- to 3-inch-long cutting from your rosemary plant.

2. Strip off the lower leaves, and strike one side of the stem with a sharp knife. Dip the bottom ¼ inch of the stem into rooting powder. (You can find rooting powder at most nurseries; however, this is an optional step.)

3. Place the cuttings into damp peat moss mixed with perlite or vermiculite. Keep the seedlings moist and in a bright spot (but not direct sunlight). Roots should develop in three to four weeks.

Give the roots a haircut. Potted rosemaries benefit from a yearly trimming of their roots so that the plant doesn't get overcrowded.

rosemaries. I should have tied branches of the tall shrubs to stakes for support. The only way to protect the prostrate plants would have been to place something over them—a bench, for instance.

Only one circumstance makes it impossible to grow these glorious plants: not enough sun. Half-day sun will produce a spindly plant, but no sun results in no rosemary at all.

Happy rosemaries are robust rosemaries that are rarely afflicted with pests. But if leaves become stippled with yellow or white specks, they probably have spider mites. If lots of leaves turn yellow and drop off, it may be whiteflies. Aphids attack dwindling plants. Spraying frequently with strong streams of water to knock off those nasties is the first step. If the problem persists, spray with insecticidal soap, following the directions on the label. Don't harvest leaves from such plants, however, until they have regained their health and are free of spray.

Rosemary is an evergreen, so it can be harvested year-round. Pick a length of 3 to 6 inches from one branch rather than shorter lengths from many tips. Pinching helps keep the plant bushy. I can't bear to prune our rosemaries, but some people cut thin branches back as much as one-half after flowering.

THIS PLANT WILL THRIVE IN POTS

Rosemary is best started with a plant from a nursery specializing in herbs or from a stem cutting of a plant you admire (see the sidebar on the facing page). When trying to choose a variety from a catalog, you may find that names and descriptions do not conform from one source to the next. No matter what the name, select the plant whose description comes closest to what you want.

To grow rosemary in pots, select potting soil with a minimum of peat moss, which is acidic, because rosemary likes an alkaline pH. Add enough sand to create good drainage. The surface should dry out between waterings, but the soil should never be completely dry.

The only disadvantage of having to bring rosemary indoors is that flowers will be sacrificed if branches must be cut back because they are formed on the previous year's growth. Indoors, rosemary needs ample light, not too much heat, good air circulation, and fairly high humidity. Spritz the plant two or three times a week.

Rosemaries don't like being transplanted and don't mind crowded roots, but they don't like to be over-crowded, either. Each spring, before new growth starts, slide the plant out of its pot and snip back the roots by one-quarter (see the photo above). Replace one-quarter of the potting mix with fresh soil. Your rosemary plant will then be ready for a new season.

CHIVES
ARE THE ULTIMATE HERB

No matter what type you grow, the good looks and delicious flavor of chives can't be beat. These easy-to-grow herbs are best fresh from the garden, so follow herbalist Susan Belsinger's advice for a season full of flavor.

I LOVE IT WHEN, IN EARLY SPRING, BRIGHT GREEN CHIVES POKE from the ground like stretching arms, bearing the news that the growing season is finally here. Later, the purple buds of the common chive pop open above the sea of green in the garden, delighting me with the first edible flowers. Then, in midsummer, the first snowy white blooms of garlic chive appear.

Flowers are only one of the reasons to grow chives. The flavor of chives, with the sweetness of an onion and the hint of new garlic, adds a pleasing touch to many dishes. Because of their versatility, chives are found in cuisines around the world. For the French, chives are an integral ingredient in classic seasoning mixes and are used to enhance all manner of egg dishes, sauces, and lightly cooked vegetables. English farmhouse cheeses often feature chives, and they are also used in sandwiches. German cooks incorporate them in sauces served with meat and fish. Italians put them in summer-greens salads and pair them with tomatoes. Pick any country in the world and chances are that cooks from that

Common chives are great tasting and beautiful, making them a welcome addition to a veggie patch or an ornamental garden.

They look and taste different. The tubular stem of the common chive on the right (top left) is vastly different than the flat stem of the garlic chive on the left. Although both kinds are attractive, garlic chives (bottom left) have a larger white blossom, and their leaves pack a pungent punch—unlike the mellow onion flavor of common chives (above).

region use chives in their cuisine, because this herb is so incredibly versatile and flavorful.

THEY'RE EASY TO GROW AND PROPAGATE

Given the appeal of this tasty herb, I was happy to discover that it doesn't need much care in the garden. I planted chives in my first herb garden many years ago, and they've been with me ever since. The slender, dark green leaves of both common and garlic chives thrive on my continual snipping for culinary pursuits. The flowers attract bees and butterflies. They attract friends, as well; I've divided and passed around chives to more gardeners than I can count.

Both the common chive and the garlic chive are hardy perennials. The common chive (*Allium schoenoprasum*, see

the right photo above) has narrow, tubular leaves 10 to 15 inches long. The flower stalks reach 18 to 24 inches tall when they bloom from mid- to late spring. The 1-inch-wide flowers are lavender when they first open, then turn to purple with a dark pink center when fully unfurled. The garlic chive (*A. tuberosum*, see the bottom left photo above) has flat, broad leaves 12 to 15 inches long, and the plant can reach 2½ feet tall when in bloom. Starting in midsummer, this showy plant produces abundant pure white umbels, with each flower cluster measuring 2 to 2½ inches across.

To get started, buy chive plants from a garden center or herb supplier or get some from a friend. Chives like average soil, good drainage, and four to six hours of sun. They don't require a lot of water—once a week if they're in the ground and there's no rain, or two or three times a week if they're in a pot. They're not bothered much by pests, either.

CHIVE BASICS

- Purchase chive plants from a nursery, or get a division from a friend.

- Plant in a spot that gets four to six hours of sun and has good drainage.

- Water once a week if the plants are in the ground and there's no rain.

- If the leaves start to yellow, divide the plants into 1-inch-diameter clumps in spring or fall.

Simply snip the base of the flowers to separate the florets into little bites of flavor.

Chives don't thrive on neglect, but it's certainly easy to keep them content. Occasional feedings of fish emulsion make them vigorous. They spread rapidly and can become overcrowded; where there's one plant at the start of the season, there will be a cluster of plants at the end. If the leaves start to yellow, divide the plants into 1-inch-diameter clumps in spring or fall.

After the summer bloom, cut chive plants all the way back to encourage new foliage. In warm climates, such as in Florida and Southern California, chives will grow year-round, albeit slowly. In colder climates, you can let the plants go dormant in the ground or move potted chives indoors onto a cool windowsill without a lot of sun.

USE THE FLOWER AND THE STEM

The refined taste of the common chive goes well with light foods, such as salads, whereas the garlic chive is assertive and good for flavoring heartier, robust dishes. Fresh chives are available in markets in spring, summer, and fall, but these chives are often a large variety with a slightly coarse flavor. Frozen fresh, snipped leaves retain good flavor for up to three months. I snip my chives into an airtight container and use them through the winter, straight from the freezer.

The flowers of these alliums are a delight to the palate as well as the eye. They taste much like the leaves, with an onionlike aroma and flavor. The flower of garlic chive is more pungent than that of common chive. When bringing flowers in from the garden, get rid of the insects outside.

Gently rinse the flowers in cool water, and pat them dry. A note of caution: Always be sure you have correctly identified the flowers you are about to eat. Know where they come from and that they haven't been treated with insecticide or other chemicals.

A chive flower is quite a mouthful, so you probably will want to separate it into florets for a more appealing size. To remove the stem and separate the florets of common chive, hold the blossom in one hand, with the stem facing out. Using a sharp pair of scissors, make a V-shaped cut deep inside the blossom, clipping on either side of the stem so that the florets fall away (see the photo above). Handle the blooms of garlic chive in the same manner, but snip straight across the individual flower stem close to the flowers to eliminate most of the stem and get mainly flowers. You can keep flowers in the refrigerator between damp paper towels for up to eight hours.

Use chive flowers anywhere you would use fresh chopped chives: to flavor butter, vinegar, sauces, soups, and vegetables. They are good with cheese and egg dishes, potatoes, and tomatoes. Use them to garnish salads, grilled meats, and fish. No matter how you prepare them, chives are always a culinary treat.

CILANTRO
SUCCESS

You, too, can have the bold flavor—and aroma—of cilantro at your fingertips. Learn the tips and tricks for making this refreshing herb go the distance from author and cook Lucinda Hutson.

CILANTRO SHOWS OFF ITS VERSATILITY IN THE KITCHEN AND IN the kitchen garden. Also known as coriander leaf and Chinese parsley, this aromatic herb is bursting with flavor. Cilantro provides a refreshing foil for the fiery chiles, garlic, and spices favored in Mexican, Chinese, Southeast Asian, and Indian foods. Cooks around the world use different parts of this plant. Thai cuisine features the roots in spicy marinades, while the bright green leaves season and garnish Chinese stir-fries and Vietnamese noodles. The leaves provide the green garnish that enlivens Mexican salsas, soups, and salads. Even cilantro's seeds—known as coriander—have international culinary appeal, and its dainty white flowers may be used as edible garnish for salads or sorbets.

While cilantro brings delight in the kitchen, it may cause gardeners despair when they attempt to grow it. Cilantro abounds in hot-blooded countries and cuisines, yet it resents hot weather. It bolts at the first sign of summer (or spring) in my Texas garden. Several unseasonably warm days will send it into a premature flowering frenzy. I learned to grow cilantro the hard way. Following

Bold flavor makes cilantro a star in many cuisines.

BELOW When the true leaves appear, thin the plants. Don't attempt to space the seedlings later on in the season because, once established, cilantro resents being moved.

ABOVE It's almost too beautiful to be in the veggie patch. Cilantro flowers resemble those of Queen Anne's lace and attract a slew of beneficial insects.

CILANTRO BASICS

- Direct-sow plants every two to three weeks, starting about two weeks before the last-frost date in cool climates.

- In warmer zones, sow in early fall and late winter.

- Thin the seedlings so that they're a foot apart, and mulch to cool the roots.

- Once the plants bolt, allow them to go to seed.

advice in British and New England gardening books, I sowed seeds in spring once there was no danger of frost. By April, I had a garden full of stunted cilantro plants in full bloom, long before their culinary partners—tomatoes, chiles, eggplant, and squash—were ready to harvest. That was before I learned several tricks for getting better production out of this amazing herb.

WHEN YOU SOW DEPENDS ON WHERE YOU LIVE

I now sow cilantro seeds in successive plantings every few weeks from early fall through late winter, assuring me a steady supply of tender greens as well as flowers. Gardeners in cooler locations should direct-sow the seeds every two to three weeks, starting about two weeks before the last-frost date. Sometimes I scatter seeds on a whim; otherwise, I sow seeds ½ inch deep, thinning the seedlings to a foot apart when their true leaves appear. I plant cilantro in several areas of my garden, using it as an edible ornamental in the flower bed as well as a staple in the kitchen garden.

When the plant is young, cilantro's glossy, finely divided flat leaves resemble those of Italian parsley. It then visibly changes in character. As the plant stretches to reach its ultimate height of 2 to 2½ feet, it appears spindly with small sparse and lacy secondary leaves. Throughout its growth, the leaves and stems of cilantro may be used. The newer, greener leaves are preferable to the feathery secondary leaves, which have a tendency to be bitter.

Those with limited garden space may choose to buy cilantro transplants from nurseries. One or two plants per

ABOVE Make the best of bolted cilantro. Be sure to collect its seeds (known as coriander), because they have an intriguing flavor all their own.

garden should be adequate. Because it has a long taproot, it should not be transplanted once it's established in the garden. With the exception of its proclivity to bolt, cilantro is a worry-free annual and virtually takes care of itself. Cilantro thrives when given ideal growing conditions—rich, loose, well-drained soil; full sun; and adequate water—but it will grow in some shade. In fact, offering cilantro some afternoon shade can prolong the season slightly.

FLOWERS SIGNAL THE ARRIVAL OF SEEDS

To my dismay, I must accept the fact that, despite my best efforts, cilantro will not last through the hottest days of summer. But before the plants die, they send up stalks of beautiful flowers, followed by tasty seeds. Cilantro's shiny coriander seeds resemble small green peppercorns. The clean, strong citrus taste of the unripened seeds is a natural breath freshener. Sprinkle them over salads, poached salmon, or grilled fish for a surprising burst of flavor. The coriander seeds ripen to a toasty brown, mellowing in flavor. They are renowned for their bittersweet bite in spice blends and baked goods, and I always add them to homemade chicken and beef stock.

Harvest the coriander seeds before they dry out in the hot sun by hanging the long flower stems of the plant

MAKE THE HARVEST LAST LONGER

- Cilantro flourishes when nights are cool and days are sunny, like those found in early spring and autumn, so planting should be confined to these times. Virtually unfazed by brief cold snaps and only slightly rumpled after a hard freeze, cilantro rallies again with renewed vigor and fresh growth at the first hint of sunshine. This plant will continue to grace the garden for several months, until the hot weather sets in.

- Offer light feedings of fish emulsion and seaweed fertilizer when first establishing the plant; continued feedings will sacrifice flavor for foliage. Applying compost and mulch around the base of the plant adds nutrients, helps retain water, and keeps the roots cool—which ultimately results in the plant living longer. Cilantro's odoriferous qualities seem to repel harmful insects, yet butterflies, ladybugs, and other beneficial insects frequently come to visit.

- Slow-bolt seeds seem to extend cilantro's productivity, sometimes giving an extra month of growth before going into flower. Although pinching off the flower heads as they emerge may deter it slightly, once cilantro has set its mind to flower, it will. Up shoots a thick purplish stalk, while the leaves become feathery and fernlike. Cutting the stalk only makes it push harder.

upside down in a paper bag in a dark, well-ventilated room. The seeds will fall off their stems when shaken. They should be stored in an airtight jar because weevils are fond of them.

Once cilantro has made a home for itself in your garden, it willingly reseeds, offering an encore of fragrance, flavor, and flowers.

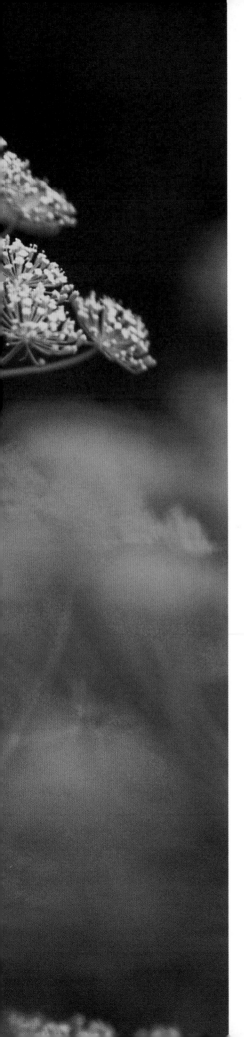

DILL'S A BREEZE

Enjoy the lush look—and culinary magic—of dill all summer long. Gardener Peter Garnham shows you how easy it is to grow. You already know how easy it is to eat.

MANY YEARS AGO, IN MY NATIVE ENGLAND, I WAS EXPLORING the tangled and sadly overgrown walled garden of an old manor house when I brushed against some self-sown dill. I knew what it was, but I had never before seen it growing. I picked some fresh leaves, returned a few weeks later to gather some seeds, and I have grown dill almost every year since. To this day, dill's wonderfully relaxing and reassuring aroma brings back a vivid memory of that Essex countryside and the softly faded beauty that was all around me. Dill leaf and dill seed work magic in the kitchen, and I love the plant's blue-green, ferny mist. To me, dill epitomizes the joy and lushness of a summer garden.

Glide through summer with this eager herb that is full of flavor.

ABOVE Though dill may be a garden featherweight, just a touch of its rich blue-green leaves in the kitchen elevates summer fare to top-shelf.

RIGHT Dill self-seeds at the drop of a hat, the papery seeds flying from their roosts in spindly tufts.

DILL DELIVERS THE LEAF QUICKLY

Given the right conditions—and the range is broad—dill grows fast. If seed, soil, and sun are on your side, you can snip mature leaves eight weeks after planting. Because I am so eager every year to taste and smell the first dill, I generally start a few dozen seedlings indoors.

This habit is almost entirely self-serving, since the direct-seeded plants mature only slightly, if at all, behind my carefully cosseted indoor seedlings. Dill puts down a slender taproot that resents being moved, and I suspect tiny root hairs get jostled and broken in transplanting. That small setback allows the undisturbed direct-seeded competition to catch up. Succession plantings three weeks apart guarantee an unbroken supply, and its fast growth allows dill to be raised from Zones 3 through 10.

Dill is a light feeder, but it does best in a reasonably fertile, open soil with full sun. Southern gardeners can even grow it in partial shade. My kitchen garden gets a top dressing of an inch or two of compost and rotted manure every year. Unless your soil lacks nutrients, dill won't require any supplemental feeding. But to maintain the general fertility of the soil, I run weak manure tea into my drip irrigation lines every two or three weeks. And after a heavy harvest of dill, you will find a quick shot of manure tea helps the plants recover.

Good drainage is essential, and my Long Island, New York, sandy loam has that advantage. Heavier clay soils should be amended with lots of compost. I loosen my dill beds with deep thrusts of a spading fork to ease the passage of those slender taproots.

Most vegetables, particularly cabbage and other cole crops, onions, and lettuce, enjoy the company of dill. Carrots, however, will grow poorly if they mix with a certain chemical in dill seeds. So it's best to keep carrots and dill far apart if you plan to let your dill self-seed.

Like other members of the Umbelliferae, dill forms flowers in a graceful umbrella shape. Getting through the stiff language and odd spellings in the 1597 book *The Herball, or Generall Historie of Plantes* was hard, but when I found author John Gerard's listing of dill I felt repaid. It has little yellow flowers "standing in a spokie tuft or rundle," he wrote.

FASTIDIOUS PLANTING IS ITS OWN REWARD

After preparation of the seedbed, I form a groove by lightly pressing down with the edge of a square stick. Rows should be 6 inches apart for leaf dill, and 1 foot apart for seed because the plants can get quite large when fully mature.

LEFT The plant sends down a slender taproot and grows vigorously. Prune back the plants after a first crop and watch a diminutive but tasty stand return in the same place.

Drip irrigation puts water where the plants need it: at their roots. Overhead watering creates a perfect environment for fungus and mildew diseases.

DILL'S TOO FAST FOR PESTS TO CATCH

Grown for its leaves, dill is usually in and out of the garden before it can attract pests. If the plant matures to the seed stage, it can be afflicted, although rarely, with tomato hornworm, aphids, or even carrot rust fly. Hornworms are big enough to be handpicked, although their camouflage makes them hard to find until your eyes get used to spotting their bulk amid the delicate ferny leaves of the dill.

Aphids are best dealt with by snipping off the affected plant, spritzing away the aphids with a spray of water, and enjoying the dill yourself. I believe that larvae of the carrot rust fly attack dill only when it is grown where carrots were grown before it. Parasitic nematodes are the best remedy.

ONE SIZE DILL MAY NOT FIT ALL

Seed catalogs offer a choice of dill varieties. 'Bouquet' has long been a favorite of commercial growers for both leaf and seed production, although many home and market gardeners prefer 'Dukat', sometimes listed as 'Tetra' dill, for its abundant and sweet foliage.

In 1997, Johnny's Selected Seeds introduced 'Super-dukat', a variety the catalog said has more essential oil than 'Dukat' and grows straighter and more uniformly for easier harvesting. It also germinated sooner and grew faster than the other four varieties in my garden.

'Long Island' or 'Mammoth' dill, different names for the same plant, is also favored by commercial growers as a reliable producer. The 'Fernleaf' variety, a 1992 All-America Selections winner, has dark blue-green foliage and resists bolting.

For me, every one of them evokes a sensory flashback to the dill that, long ago, haunted a forgotten English garden with its lovely aroma.

Dill seeds are fairly small, and they tend to clump together, so I mix them with a little dry sand; this separates them and makes it easier to get a thin, even distribution of seeds along the row. The seeds should be lightly covered with ¼ in to ½ inch of sifted soil, then firmed and watered in. Germination takes about 10 days. You may want to thin plants to 2 to 6 inches apart, depending on soil fertility.

For all this pedantic care, I must confess I have had equally good results in the rich soil of my market garden using an EarthWay® seeder to sow unthinned 100-foot-long rows that are 6 inches apart. But like most gardeners, I suspect, the pleasure I get from gentling the seeds into the soil of my home kitchen garden is its own reward.

Germination requires an uninterrupted supply of moisture. Long an advocate of drip irrigation, I lay strips of drip hose about a foot apart. The emitters are also a foot apart, and in my soil this gives adequate coverage.

8

VEGGIE VARIETIES

BEANS & PEAS

'AMETHYST' BEAN
Phaseolus vulgaris **'Amethyst'**

Expect longer (more than 5 inches) and straighter beans than its predecessor, 'Royal Burgundy', but with the same crisp flavor. The vigorous vines will need sturdy supports.

—*FINE GARDENING* EDITORS

'CHRISTMAS' LIMA BEAN
Phaseolus lunatus **'Christmas'**

This heirloom variety is known for its large (quarter-size) white beans with maroon swirls. But the tall vining plant is attractive, as well, with its heart-shaped leaves and white blooms in late summer. The foliage, as lush as it is, is not able to hide the heavy yields of 4- to 6-inch-long pods, which can reach 1 inch in width.

—KEITH CROTZ

'Christmas' lima bean

'PINKEYE PURPLE HULL' COWPEA
Vigna unguiculata **'Pinkeye Purple Hull'**

'Pinkeye Purple Hull' cowpea loves the South's hot summers and can tolerate dry weather as long as it receives some water when blooming. The pods turn purple when ripe, so that's an easy indicator of when to harvest. I pick them every three or four days to encourage more blooming and to get the biggest yield. A typical yield is about one bushel per 100-foot-long row.

—SIMON BEVIS

'Pinkeye Purple Hull' cowpea

'TRUE RED CRANBERRY' BEAN
Phaseolus vulgaris **'True Red Cranberry'**

This is a pole bean that should be dried and used in similar fashion as the common kidney bean. Most describe the flavor as being nutty and rich. These beans originated in Maine, where they were served in cooking shacks that floated on rivers. It's there that they were possibly mistaken as cranberries from nearby bogs.

—*FINE GARDENING* EDITORS

CORN

'MIRAI® CORN'
Zea mays **Mirai**

Mirai is not only supersweet but also wonderfully tender. Direct-sow the seed after the soil has warmed up to at least 65°F. If you're growing more than one kind of corn, avoid cross-pollination by planting Mirai two weeks later than the other corn. This hybrid should be given a bit more space between plants than other varieties, and the seed should be sown 1½ inches deep.

—TERI SMITH

'Mirai' corn

'ROY'S CALAIS FLINT' CORN
Zea mays **'Roy's Calais Flint'**

Originally from Vermont, this variety is said to be the only corn type to survive the record low temperatures during the infamous "Year Without a Summer" in 1816. The 7-foot-tall plants produce 8- to 12-inch-long ears that are golden yellow or maroon red. The kernels are perfect for grinding into cornmeal.

—*FINE GARDENING* EDITORS

CUCUMBERS

'CRYSTAL APPLE' CUCUMBER
Cucumis sativus **'Crystal Apple'**

The tender white fruits of 'Crystal Apple' are said to have a mild flavor, making them a favorite of folks who have digestive issues with the standard green varieties. This selection is similar to the heirloom 'Lemon' cucumber, but you can expect more fruit from its prolific vines.

—*FINE GARDENING* EDITORS

'NIPPON SANJAKU KIURI' CUCUMBER
Cucumis sativus 'Nippon Sanjaku Kiuri'

Its name translates to "Japanese three-foot cucumber," and the narrow fruit will get that big, if you let them. For the sweetest flavor, however, you should pick them when they are 18 inches long. Excellent for fresh eating and pickling, these disease-resistant plants need to be trellised.

—FINE GARDENING EDITORS

EGGPLANTS

'DIAMOND' EGGPLANT
Solanum melongena 'Diamond'

'Diamond' is a typical oval, Japanese-style purple eggplant from Ukraine that begins delivering in early July and continues copious production right up to frost. Eight to 10 plants yield a wheelbarrow of fruit by season's end—plenty enough for fresh eating all summer as well as an ample supply of roasted, peeled flesh for the freezer.

—DAVID CAVAGNARO

'Diamond' eggplant

'PINGTUNG LONG' EGGPLANT
Solanum melongena 'Pingtung'

The beautiful lavender fruit, which grows 11 inches long and 2 inches across, is tender and sweet. Sow seeds indoors eight weeks prior to transplanting. Plant the seedlings 18 inches apart. Use a floating row cover to minimize damage by flea beetles.

—DAVE LLEWELLYN

'Pingtung Long' eggplant

GREENS

'BRIGHT LIGHTS' CHARD
Beta vulgaris subsp. Cicla var. flavescens 'Bright Lights'

A veggie that is almost as pretty as it is tasty, 'Bright Lights' chard produces voluptuous leaves throughout the year. The stems can be red, pink, gold, orange, or white. Some can even be striped. The flavor is similar to spinach.

—CAREY THORNTON

'CARETAKER' LETTUCE
Lactuca Sativa 'Caretaker'

It's an iceberg variety that thrives in the heat and humidity. The average-size heads are slow to bolt and do not easily get tip burn (common among iceberg types).

—FINE GARDENING EDITORS

'GEORGIA' COLLARD
Brassica oleracea 'Georgia'

Collard grows well in the mild winters of the coastal plains, and in spring and fall in other parts of the South. It is a member of the Brassicaceae along with cabbage, kale, and broccoli, and it requires similar growing conditions. The plants can grow more than 2 feet tall in fertile soils, so don't plant them too close together. Larger outside leaves can be harvested while the younger leaves mature for an extended harvest.

—SIMON BEVIS

'Georgia' collard

'RED MALABAR' SPINACH
Basella alba 'Red Malabar'

This beautiful Asian green is a great summer substitute for traditional spinach. The fleshy green leaves and attractive red stems are high in vitamins A and C. Be aware that germination is slow—10 to 12 days at 80°F—so start the seed indoors three to six weeks before transplanting outside. "Red Malabar" spinach needs trellising; in fact, I like to plant mine next to pea trellises and let it take over as the peas finish up.

—IRA WALLACE

'Red Malabar' spinach

'SPECKLED AMISH' LETTUCE
Lactuca sativa 'Speckled Amish'

This head lettuce always earns compliments in the field for its beauty. It is a stunning, light green Bibb lettuce with maroon flecks. The flavor is a light, sweet complement to any companion in your salad bowl. Its one flaw is a tendency to burn at its tips in higher temperatures, so consider using a shade cloth in summer.

—DAVE LLEWELLYN

'Speckled Amish' lettuce

HERBS

'BERGGARTEN' SAGE
Salvia officinalis 'Berggarten'

This is my favorite sage because of its wide but dignified girth. Eating the substantial leaves is a pleasure because they aid in digestion. The whole stem can be used in ornamental bouquets or as a garnish for the Thanksgiving bird. Like most sages, 'Berggarten' hates wet feet.

—ANNE DUNCAN

'CAESAR' BASIL
Ocimum basilicum 'Caesar'

It doesn't bolt as fast as traditional varieties, like 'Genovese', and produces lots of large leaves on shorter, more compact plants.

—FINE GARDENING EDITORS

'LISETTE' PARSLEY
Petroselinum crispum 'Lisette'

Better than the well-known cultivar 'Moss Curled' because it has better heat tolerance, this variety can be enjoyed throughout the entire season. Its tight, compact habit (reaching only 8 to 10 inches tall and wide) makes it suitable for any size space.

—FINE GARDENING EDITORS

'MRS. BURNS' LEMON BASIL
Ocimum basilicum 'Mrs. Burns'

There are lots of lemon basils to choose from, but 'Mrs. Burns' is the best because it has not only large leaves with excellent lemon flavor but also all the spiciness of regular basil. This herb can get more than 3 feet tall and is topped with spires of pink flowers in summer. Cut off the flowers for increased leaf production.

—ANNE DUNCAN

'CREEPING' ROSEMARY
Rosmarinus officinalis 'Prostratus'

An atypical option, trailing rosemary trails across the ground or over the edge of containers and walls. It's a fantastic spiller that pairs well with other herbs. In areas where trailing rosemary is a hardy shrub, the cascading branches can grow to be several feet long. Hold off on pruning until just after plants have flowered in early summer. Trailing rosemary requires good drainage.

—JENNIFER BENNER

'Creeping' Rosemary

'PURPUREUM' BRONZE FENNEL
Foeniculum vulgare 'Purpureum'

The lacy bronze foliage of this fragrant herb contrasts against most other garden companions, especially when the herb's bright yellow flowers bloom. Bees and butterflies flock to this plant when it's in flower. The stems and foliage are gorgeous in cut-flower arrangements. All fennels are easily grown from seed.

—ANNE DUNCAN

'RED RUBIN' BASIL
Ocimim basilicum var. *purpurascens* 'Red Rubin'

Unlike common sweet basil, 'Red Rubin' sports a deep purple-red color. The flavor of 'Red Rubin' and other purple-red plants is milder than that of traditional green basil, but they still make a good addition to salads and vinaigrettes. To prevent disease problems, give plants good air circulation and water them at the base (not on their leaves). Also, stay on top of deadheading; basil leaves begin to taste bitter when plants are allowed to flower.

—JENNIFER BENNER

'TRICOLOR' SAGE
Salvia officinalis 'Tricolor'

'Tricolor' sage's leaves, decorated with splashes of cream and a flush of purple, make it easy to create pleasing plant combos. No matter what you pair with this sage, be sure to plant it in a spot with good drainage; too much moisture—especially over winter—will kill it. This species is, in fact, fairly tolerant of drought conditions and poor soil.

—JENNIFER BENNER

VARIEGATED OREGANO
Origanum vulgare 'Variegatum'

Variegated oregano gives plantings a new twist on an herbal favorite with its attractive pale yellow leaf mar-

Variegated oregano

gins. The leaves are slightly less peppery than common oregano but are still flavorful and a worthy culinary ingredient. Oregano is happy to be on the dry side and in rocky soil.

—JENNIFER BENNER

VARIEGATED LEMON THYME
Thymus x citriodorus 'Variegatus'

The cultivar 'Variegatus' has tiny leaves rimmed in gold that look great spilling over the edge of a pot or walkway. It has the same strong lemony scent and pleasant flavor as lemon thyme, and it's used in all sorts of foods—from breads to vinegars to meat dishes.

—JENNIFER BENNER

ONIONS

'RED CREOLE' ONION
Allium cepa 'Red Creole'

These red-skinned, white-fleshed globes boast a sharp flavor that is tasty but not overwhelming. Resistant to pink-root disease, 'Red Creole' can be stored and enjoyed for up to seven months if properly cured.

—FINE GARDENING EDITORS

'TADORNA' LEEK
Allium porrum 'Tadorna'

'Tadorna' has a long white shaft and holds better in the field than any other variety I have grown. Typically you'll get about 1 pound of leeks per foot.

—MIKE PERONI

PEPPERS

'CHERRY STUFFER' PEPPER
Capsicum annuum 'Cherry Stuffer'

It's got the same round shape and juicy flesh of a cherry pepper, but

it's sweet. Short, compact plants produce scores of perfectly shaped peppers from midsummer until fall. The thin skin of the fruit makes it perfect for roasting or skewering with kebabs.

—FINE GARDENING EDITORS

'FEHEROZON' PEPPER
Capsicum annuum 'Feherozon'

My sweet pepper of choice for fresh eating, cooking, and freezing is 'Feherozon'. It's a pointed, pimento-type Hungarian pepper that starts out yellow and turns orange-red when ripe. The small plants are often so loaded with big peppers that one can hardly see the leaves.

—DAVID CAVAGNARO

'Feherozon' pepper

'GYPSY' PEPPER
Capsicum annuum 'Gypsy'

With its delicious and prolific fruit, this pepper should be on the top of every gardener's list. This variety has especially sturdy stems that will not bend or break when strong wind come sweeping in. 'Gypsy' pepper sets fruit all summer long and does not give out when the heavy heat of summer sets in. Its thin walls mean that fruit mature to red nearly twice as fast as other

'Gypsy' pepper

'Santa Fe Grande' pepper

'KENNEBEC' POTATO
Solanum tuberosum 'Kennebec'

'Kennebec' originated in Maine and is adaptable to a wide range of soil conditions. Its resistance to late blight makes it even more attractive. Once the plants reach 6 inches tall, hill the plants with soil and repeat as they grow taller. Keep the plants well watered.

—DAVE LLEWELLYN

'YUKON GOLD' POTATO
Solanum tuberosum 'Yukon Gold'

Golden from the inside out, this tuber has a sweet taste and creamy texture. 'Yukon Gold' is known for low yields, but its early nature and long-storing ability make it a top pick.

—SHAIN SABERON

peppers. Early harvests mean fewer culls from disease and hungry garden critters, and thick foliage protects the plants from being burned by the sun.

—MIKE APPEL & EMILY OAKLEY

'PEACEWORK' BELL PEPPER
Capsicum annuum 'Peacework'

This red bell pepper was bred for the Northeast to be sweet and early. Sow seeds indoors in late March, and set seedlings out after the danger of frost has passed. Plant them about 12 inches apart.

—DAVE LLEWELLYN

'SANTA FE GRANDE' PEPPER
Capsicum annuum 'Santa Fe Grande'

Mildly spicy, this heirloom pepper thrives in the heat of southwestern summers. 'Santa Fe Grande' can be direct-seeded or transplanted. To germinate in the ground, seeds will need warm soil and air. To start producing fruit, the plant needs really hot temperatures. It produces high yields of 4-inch-long peppers throughout the growing season and is an excellent pepper for roasting.

—ERIC LUTHER

POTATOES

'CENTENNIAL' SWEET POTATO
Ipomoea batatas 'Centennial'

Sweet potatoes require a longer growing season than most other vegetables, often taking as much as four months for the root to reach full maturity. 'Centennial' is an excellent choice for anyone who doesn't want to wait that long, because it reaches maturity a bit faster than other varieties. The plants can spread up to 10 feet, so be sure to give them room.

—KEITH CROTZ

'Kennebec' potato

SQUASH

'BURGESS BUTTERCUP' WINTER SQUASH
Cucurbita maxima 'Burgess Buttercup'

Most of the top-flavored and top-textured squash belong to the species *Cucurbita maxima*, and 'Burgess Buttercup' ranks among the best. Its medium-size fruit are a manageable

'Burgess Buttercup' winter squash

size for most families. It will keep well over the winter, yet its skin is tender enough for easy cutting. It's excellent for baking, and once you've used this squash to make a pie, you will never go back to pumpkin.

—DAVID CAVAGNARO

'GOLDEN EGG' SQUASH
Cucurbita pepo 'Golden Egg'

Creamy, sweet flesh is what earned 'Golden Egg' a medal in Burpee's taste trials for two years in a row. This squash tastes nothing like a traditional summer squash. A bush variety, 'Golden Egg' will still vine 2 to 3 feet but is more manageable than other squash plants.

—*FINE GARDENING* EDITORS

'GREEN STRIPED CUSHAW' WINTER SQUASH
Cucurbita mixta 'Green Striped Cushaw'

A Native American heirloom, 'Green Striped Cushaw' is a huge, vigorous vine, so give it plenty of room when planting. If the fruits are exposed to a cold snap, their thick, pale orange flesh will become sweeter. Fruits weigh 5 pounds on average but can get as heavy as 20 pounds. They store well at cooler room temperatures, gaining flavor through the winter.

—ERIC LUTHER

'Green Striped Cushaw' winter squash

'MR. WRINKLES' PUMPKIN
Cucurbita pepo 'Mr. Wrinkles'

In the vegetable world, when fruit is large, it generally means that a plant won't be very productive. It's not the case, though, with this pumpkin. These vines yield tons of 20- to 30-pound fruits that are deeply grooved and barrel shaped (giving them perfect jack-o'-lantern potential). Be sure to give 'Mr. Wrinkles' room to grow, because the plants can scramble up to 120 feet.

—*FINE GARDENING* EDITORS

TOMATOES

'BISON' GLOBE TOMATO
Solanum lycopersicum 'Bison'

This variety thrives in adversity of all kinds, from drought and floods to high winds and extreme temperature fluctuations. It sets copious amounts of fruit early. Even though the flavor isn't the best (low acid and sugar), it can be improved by a sprinkle of sugar or salt.

—AMY GOLDMAN

'Bison' globe tomato

'BLACK KRIM' GLOBE TOMATO
Solanum lycopersicum 'Black Krim'

The violet-brown fruits of this medium-size tomato have raspberry-colored flesh that is exceptionally juicy. Some people describe the flavor as smoky.

—AMY GOLDMAN

'Black Krim' globe tomato

'BROWN BERRY' CHERRY TOMATO
Solanum lycopersicum 'Brown Berry'

This tomato tastes so good that you'll never want to grow a red cherry variety again. The reasonably firm, crack-resistant fruits hold up well under myriad growing conditions.

—AMY GOLDMAN

'Brown Berry' cherry tomato

'GOLDMAN'S ITALIAN AMERICAN' PLUM TOMATO

Solanum lycopersicum 'Goldman's Italian American'

This voluptuous, rich red tomato makes the creamiest sauce imaginable. It matures in 66 to 80 days.

—AMY GOLDMAN

'GOLD RUSH CURRANT' CURRANT TOMATO

Solanum lycopersicum 'Gold Rush Currant'

'Gold Rush Currant' is a supersweet, small-fruiting tomato. The plant can be unwieldy and staking is almost impossible, but the tomato's candy-like flavor is worth the effort.

—AMY GOLDMAN

'Gold Rush Currant' currant tomato

'GREEN ZEBRA' GLOBE TOMATO

Solanum lycopersicum 'Green Zebra'

The lemon-lime coloring is indicative of this tomato's flavor, and its crazy appearance will have your neighbors talking.

—AMY GOLDMAN

'Green Zebra' globe tomato

'RIESENTRAUBE' CHERRY TOMATO

Solanum lycopersicum 'Riesentraube'

It's no surprise that the name of this tomato translates to "giant bunches of grapes." The fruit sets in large sprays in midsummer, and although only 10 to 20 percent of the flowers turn into tomatoes, it's still enough to call this a high-yield variety.

—AMY GOLDMAN

'Riesentraube' cherry tomato

'SUDDUTH'S BRANDYWINE' BEEFSTEAK TOMATO

Solanum lycopersicum 'Sudduth's Brandywine'

This tomato has a rich flavor and a rich history. This pink globe has grabbed the limelight like no other for its meaty juiciness. Fruits often approach 2 pounds each. It is not the same as the original 'Brandywine' introduced in 1889 but, rather, a family heirloom from Tennessee.

—AMY GOLDMAN

'Sudduth's Brandywine' beefsteak tomato

'WAPSIPINICON PEACH' GLOBE TOMATO

Solanum lycopersicum 'Wapsipinicon Peach'

If a tomato and a peach mated, this would be their progeny. The 2- to 3-inch-long fruits are covered in fuzz, and the flesh tastes like a lemony grape. As a bonus, this plant is extremely resistant to rot.

—AMY GOLDMAN

'Wapsipinicon Peach' globe tomato

USDA HARDINESS ZONE MAP

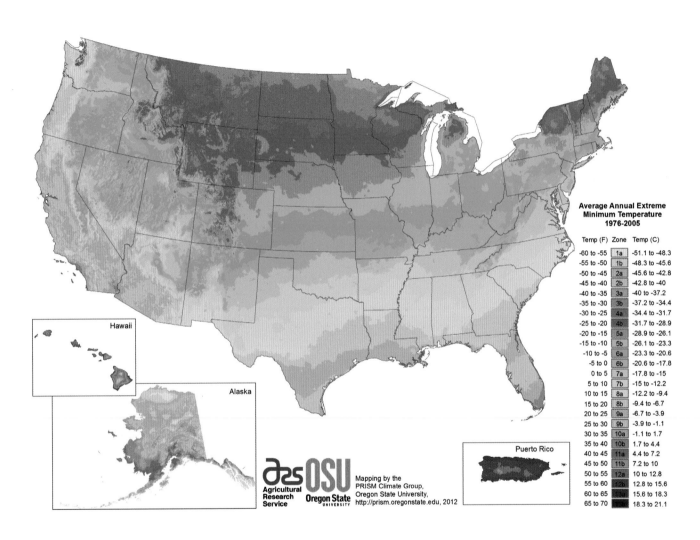

Average Annual Extreme Minimum Temperature 1976-2005

Temp (F)	Zone	Temp (C)
-60 to -55	1a	-51.1 to -48.3
-55 to -50	1b	-48.3 to -45.6
-50 to -45	2a	-45.6 to -42.8
-45 to -40	2b	-42.8 to -40
-40 to -35	3a	-40 to -37.2
-35 to -30	3b	-37.2 to -34.4
-30 to -25	4a	-34.4 to -31.7
-25 to -20	4b	-31.7 to -28.9
-20 to -15	5a	-28.9 to -26.1
-15 to -10	5b	-26.1 to -23.3
-10 to -5	6a	-23.3 to -20.6
-5 to 0	6b	-20.6 to -17.8
0 to 5	7a	-17.8 to -15
5 to 10	7b	-15 to -12.2
10 to 15	8a	-12.2 to -9.4
15 to 20	8b	-9.4 to -6.7
20 to 25	9a	-6.7 to -3.9
25 to 30	9b	-3.9 to -1.1
30 to 35	10a	-1.1 to 1.7
35 to 40	10b	1.7 to 4.4
40 to 45	11a	4.4 to 7.2
45 to 50	11b	7.2 to 10
50 to 55	12a	10 to 12.8
55 to 60	12b	12.8 to 15.6
60 to 65	13a	15.6 to 18.3
65 to 70	13b	18.3 to 21.1

Hawaii

Alaska

Puerto Rico

Agricultural Research Service

OSU Oregon State UNIVERSITY

Mapping by the PRISM Climate Group, Oregon State University, http://prism.oregonstate.edu, 2012

Those gardening in Canada should refer to the Plant Hardiness Zone Map created by the Canadian Forest Service, which can be found online at http://planthardiness.gc.ca.

METRIC EQUIVALENTS

Inches	Centimeters	Millimeters	Inches	Centimeters	Millimeters
⅛	0.3	3	13	33.0	330
¼	0.6	6	14	35.6	356
⅜	1.0	10	15	38.1	381
½	1.3	13	16	40.6	406
⅝	1.6	16	17	43.2	432
¾	1.9	19	18	45.7	457
⅞	2.2	22	19	48.3	483
1	2.5	25	20	50.8	508
1¼	3.2	32	21	53.3	533
1½	3.8	38	22	55.9	559
1¾	4.4	44	23	58.4	584
2	5.1	51	24	61.0	610
2½	6.4	64	25	63.5	635
3	7.6	76	26	66.0	660
3½	8.9	89	27	68.6	686
4	10.2	102	28	71.1	711
4½	11.4	114	29	73.7	737
5	12.7	127	30	76.2	762
6	15.2	152	31	78.7	787
7	17.8	178	32	81.3	813
8	20.3	203	33	83.8	838
9	22.9	229	34	86.4	864
10	25.4	254	35	88.9	889
11	27.9	279	36	91.4	914
12	30.5	305			

RESOURCES

GARDENING PUBLICATIONS FROM THE TAUNTON PRESS

Visit our Web site:
Tauntonstore.com
Fine Gardening magazine:
finegardening.com

Among the many books and special publications on gardening are:

Taunton's Complete Guide to Growing Vegetables and Herbs, from the publishers of *Fine Gardening* and *Kitchen Gardener*

The Pruning Book, by Lee Reich

The Gardener's Guide to Common Sense Pest Control, by Dr. William Olkowski, Sheila Daar, and Helga Olkowski

Fine Gardening's Beds & Borders, Pocket Gardens, and *Small-Space Gardening,* from the editors of *Fine Gardening*

PLANTS AND SEEDS

The following mail-order plant sellers and seed companies offer the widest selection of the plants featured in this book.

PLANTS

Annie's Annuals and Perennials
Richmond, CA; 888-266-4370
www.anniesannuals.com

Arrowhead Alpines
Fowlerville, MI; 517-223-3581
www.arrowheadalpines.com

Broken Arrow Nursery
Hamden, CT; 203-288-1026
www.brokenarrownursery.com

Forestfarm Nursery
Williams, OR; 541-846-7269
www.forestfarm.com

Garden Crossings
Zeeland, MI; 616-875-6355
www.gardencrossings.com

Nature Hills Nursery
Omaha, NE; 888-864-7663
www.naturehills.com

Plant Delights
Raleigh, NC; 919-772-4794
www.plantdelights.com

Rarefind Nursery
Jackson, NJ; 732-833-0613
www.rarefindnursery.com

Sandy Mush Herb Nursery
Leicester, NC; 828-683-2014
www.sandymushherbs.com

Stark Bro's
Louisiana, MO; 800-325-4180
www.starkbros.com

Wayside Gardens
Hodges, SC; 800-845-1124
www.waysidegardens.com

Well-Sweep Herb Farm
Port Murray, NJ
908-852-5390
www.wellsweep.com

SEEDS

Botanical Interests
Broomfield, CO; 877-821-4340
www.botanicalinterests.com

Fedco Seeds
Waterville, ME; 207-426-9900
www.fedcoseeds.com

Harris Seeds
Rochester, NY; 800-544-7938
www.harrisseeds.com

Henry Field's Seeds & Nursery Co.
Aurora, IN; 513-354-1494
www.henryfields.com

Johnny's Selected Seeds
Winslow, ME; 877-564-6697
www.johnnyseeds.com

Park Seed Co.
Hodges, SC; 800-845-3369
www.parkseed.com

Pase Seeds
North Collins, NY
716-337-0361
www.paseseeds.com

Reimer Seeds
Saint Leonard, MD
www.reimerseeds.com

Renee's Garden
Felton, CA; 888-880-7228
www.reneesgarden.com

Sand Hill Preservation Center
Calamus, IA; 563-246-2299
www.sandhillpreservation.com

Seed Savers Exchange
Decorah, IA; 563-382-5990
www.seedsavers.org

Seeds of Change
Rancho Dominguez, CA
888-762-7333
www.seedsofchange.com

Southern Exposure Seed Exchange
Mineral, VA
540-894-9480
www.southernexposure.com

St. Clare Heirloom Seeds
PO Box 556, Gillett, WI
www.stclareseeds.com

Territorial Seed Company
Cottage Grove, OR
800-626-0866
www.territorialseed.com

The Thyme Garden
Alsea, OR
541-487-8671
www.thymegarden.com

W. Atlee Burpee & Co.
Warminster, PA; 800-888-1447
www.burpee.com

NATIONAL CHAINS WITH EXTENSIVE OFFERINGS FOR GARDENERS

Agway
www.agway.com

Home Depot
www.homedepot.com

Lowes
www.lowes.com

CONTRIBUTORS

Mike Appel and Emily Oakley own and operate Three Springs Farm in Oaks, Oklahoma.

Melinda Bateman farms in Arroyo Seco, New Mexico.

Susan Belsinger is a culinary herbalist and educator in Brookeville, Maryland. She also is a contributing blogger for www.vegetablegardener.com.

Jennifer Benner, horticulturist and coauthor of *The Nonstop Garden*, is an avid herb gardener in northwest Connecticut.

Simon Bevis owns and operates Noah Valley Farm in Jacksonville, Alabama.

William Brown, a former market gardener, lives north of Indianapolis, Indiana.

David Cavagnaro has trialed over 15,000 heirloom vegetables for Seed Savers Exchange in Decorah, Iowa.

Carrie Chalmers is an organic gardener on Quoyburray Farm in Weston, Vermont.

Leslie Clapp lives in Blue Hill, Maine, where she gardens on 10 acres for eight months of the year.

Keith Crotz is chairman of Seed Savers Exchange and grows beans on his family's centennial farm in Chillicothe, Illinois.

Leonard Diggs is the manager of Shone Farm in Forestville, California.

Anne Duncan is the owner of The Salem Herbfarm in Salem, Connecticut.

Alice Krinsky Formiga formerly worked as the head gardener at Shepherd's trial garden in Litchfield, Connecticut.

Peter Garnham is a market gardener in East Hampton, New York.

Edward Giobbi is a painter, sculptor, and cookbook author. He grows much of his family's food at his home in Katonah, New York.

Sam Gittings gardens in Napa, California.

Amy Goldman grows hundreds of different varieties of heirloom vegetables in her gardens in Rhinebeck, New York, and is the author of *The Heirloom Tomato: From Garden to Table* and *The Complete Squash: A Passionate Grower's Guide to Pumpkins, Squashes, and Gourds.*

David Hirsch is the author of *The Moosewood Restaurant Kitchen Garden.* He lives and gardens near Ithaca, New York.

Alex Hitt and his wife, Betsy, are full-time farmers in Eli Whitney, North Carolina.

Cynthia Hizer grows in her market garden in Covington, Georgia.

Lucinda Hutson is an author, cook, and lecturer who gardens in Austin, Texas.

Lee James and her brother, Wayne, own Tierra Vegetables in Healdsburg, California.

Lucy Apthorp Leske lives and gardens on the island of Nantucket, Massachusetts.

Ruth Lively is a cook and gardener in New Haven, Connecticut, who has a special interest in antique vegetable varieties.

Dave Llewellyn farms for the Glynwood Center in Cold Spring, New York, where he lives with his wife and daughter.

Mimi Luebbermann, author of *My Garden: A Five-Year Journal*, gardens in Petaluma, California.

Eric Luther runs Desert Greens, a community supported agriculture farm in Las Cruces, New Mexico.

Kathy Martin has been growing vegetables for 20 years in her extensive gardens near Boston, Massachusetts.

Laura McGrath is a garden designer who lives near Boston, Massachusetts.

Jo Meller and Jim Sluyter started Five Springs Farm, a CSA farm in Bear Lake, Michigan, in 1994.

Patti Moreno is an urban, organic vegetable gardener in Roxbury, Massachusetts. Visit her Web site on sustainable gardening at www.gardengirls.com.

Mike Peroni owns and operates Boistfort Valley Farm in Curtis, Washington.

Cass Peterson runs Flickerville Mountain Farm, a market garden in southern Pennsylvania.

Joe Queirolo is garden manager at Crow Canyon Gardens, a demonstration kitchen garden in San Ramon, California.

Sandra B. Rubino tends her courtyard garden in Pensacola, Florida, with one eye out for hurricanes.

Shain Saberon and his wife, Tara, own EverGreen Farm in Star Valley, Wyoming.

Teri Smith and her husband own Smith's Acres, a 35-acre farm and garden center in Niantic, Connecticut.

Brandi Spade is a former associate editor of *Fine Gardening* who loves potatoes almost as much as she loves shoes.

Sylvia Thompson is a former contributing editor of *Kitchen Gardener* magazine.

Carey Thornton is an educator at Seattle Tilth, a nonprofit organic-gardening and urban-ecology organization in Seattle, Washington.

Chip Tynan works for the William T. Kemper Center for Home Gardening at the Missouri Botanical Garden in St. Louis, Missouri.

Ira Wallace coordinates variety selection and trials as well as seed-grower contracts at Southern Exposure Seed Exchange in Mineral, Virginia.

Kris Wetherbee grows 20 varieties of tomatoes every year at Camelot Farm in western Oregon.

Diane Ott Whealy is the cofounder of Seed Savers Exchange in Decorah, Iowa.

Nan Wishner now harvests kale year-round on a 17-acre farm in northern California.

CREDITS

(continued on p. 214)

(continued from p. 213)

pp. 96-99: Photos by Saxon Holt

pp. 100-103: Photos by Jennifer Benner

pp. 104-106: Photos by Janet M. Jemmott

p. 107: Photo by Lynn Karlin

pp. 108-109: Photos by Janet M. Jemmott

p. 110: Photo by Skye Chalmers

p. 112: Photo by Kerry Anne Moore

p. 113: Photos by Boyd Hagen

p. 114: Photos by Jefferson Kolle

p. 115: Photo by Krista Hicks Benson

pp. 116-117: Photos by Skye Chalmers

p. 118: Photo by Boyd Hagen

p. 120: Photos by Ruth Lively (top left), Boyd Hagen (top right)

p. 121: Photo by Boyd Hagen

p. 122: Photo by Victor Schrager

p. 124: Photo by Scott Phillips

pp. 126-128: Photos by Boyd Hagen

p. 129: Photos by Chip Tynan

p. 130: Photo by Janet M. Jemmott

p. 132: Illustration by Christopher Clapp

pp. 133-135: John Bray

pp. 136-141: Photos by Victor Schrager

pp. 142-147: Photos by Marc Vassallo; Illustration by Chuck Lockhart

p. 148: Photo by Marc Vassallo

pp. 150-153: Photos by Boyd Hagen

pp. 154-159: Photos by Marc Vassallo

pp. 160-163: Photos by Cary Hazlegrove

pp. 164-167: Photos by Danielle Sherry

p. 168: Photo by Graham Rice/ GardenPhotos.com

pp. 170-171: Photos by *Fine Gardening* staff

pp. 172-175: Photos by *Fine Gardening* staff

p. 176: Photo by Carry Hazlegrove

pp. 178-181: Photos by Jennifer Benner

p. 182: Photo by Boyd Hagen

pp. 184-187: Photos by Janet M. Jemmott

p. 188: Photo by Judy White/ GardenPhotos.com

pp. 190-191: Photos by Andre Baranowski

p. 192: Photos by Garca Victoris

pp. 194-195: Photos by Cary Hazlegrove

pp. 196-199: Photos by David Cavagnaro

p. 202: Photos by David Cavagnaro (left), Cozy Cabin Nursery (center), Danielle Sherry (right)

p. 203: Photos by David Cavagnaro (left and center), Danielle Sherry (right)

p. 204: Photos by Danielle Sherry (top left), David Cavagnaro (bottom left), DoreenWynja.com (right)

p. 205: Photos by Millettephotomedia.com (left), David Cavagnaro (right)

p. 206: Photos by Steven Cominsky (left), David Cavagnaro (center and right)

pp. 207: Photos by David Cavagnaro (left), *Fine Gardening* staff (center and right)

p. 208: Photos by *Fine Gardening* staff

p. 209: Map courtesy USDA

INDEX

Numbers in bold indicate pages with illustrations.

If you like this book, you'll love *Fine Gardening*.

 Taunton